Aberdeenshire Library and Information Service
www.aberdeenshire.gov.uk/libraries
Renewals Hotline 01224 661511

1 3 JUN 2012

1 4 JUN 2012

1 3 NOV 20

HEADQUARTERS

1 2 JUN 2013

ABERDEENSHIRE
LIBRARIES

WITHDRAWN
FROM LIBRARY

2 0 DEC 2013

1 4 APR 2014

2 7 FEB 2015

RENOUF-MULLER

HOW TO SPIN!

LILI

D1512766

ABERDEENSHIRE LIBRARIES

1904719

746.
12

Published in January 2012 by

Low-Impact Living Initiative
Redfield Community,
Winslow, Bucks, MK18 3LZ, UK
+44 (0)1296 714184

lili@lowimpact.org
www.lowimpact.org

Copyright © 2012 Janet Renouf-Miller

ISBN: 978-0-9566751-0-1

Editor: Elaine Koster
Photos: Lee Renouf-Miller
Illustration: Mike Hammer
Design and Layout: Commercial Campaigns Ltd

Printed in Great Britain by:
Lightning Source UK Ltd, Milton Keynes

contents

illustrations

about the author

Janet works from home, earning a living by writing and teaching spinning and knitting. She also creates hand-dyed yarns for sale and sells hand woven scarves to galleries.

Spinning for at least ten minutes a day helps keep her calm and focused and she uses it as a form of meditation.

Having learned to knit at the age of six, Janet had become bored with it, until one day she saw someone spinning. Rushing home, she tried it with a hand spindle made from a pencil and a potato and was amazed when it worked. The rest, as they say, is history and in 1995 she studied for the Certificate of Achievement in Handspinning and became a spinning teacher.

Since then, Janet has taught many people to spin, crochet, knit and dye and has never stopped knitting again.

She is a registered teacher with the Association of Weavers Spinners and Dyers and has taught at their renowned Summer School. Janet has also taught courses for many spinning and weaving Guilds, knitting groups, shops and voluntary organisations.

Her booklets on spinning, dyeing and knitting have proved popular with students on her courses and this, her first book, is a natural progression.

Campaigning about environmental issues has played a significant part in Janet's life. She was chair of Ayrshire Friends of the Earth for many years and also served on the Board of Friends of the Earth Scotland in the past.

She was particularly delighted to be asked to write a book for LILI, having respected their work for some time.

With her husband Lee she moved from the country into a nearby village with amenities ten years ago, in order to develop a more sustainable and simpler lifestyle. They both work part time and have a lifestyle with very low overheads, meaning there is time to have a lot more fun!

They grow a surprising amount of food in an average-sized if vertically-challenged garden and are WWOOF (Worldwide Opportunities on Organic Farms) hosts. Their house has solar panels and a wood burning stove.

introduction

This book is about how to spin yarn: but not only that. It looks at the wide choice of fibres available and helps you to choose the right spinning tool for you.

There are choices to make about what to spin and how to spin it and these decisions impact upon the planet in different ways. Whether this is of interest or not will depend on the reasons you want to spin. If you *do* want to limit your impact, as many spinners do, there is some information to help you.

There are numerous types of fibre available for spinners and many of these are explored. Some are from animals, such as wool, Alpaca, camel and silk. Some from plants like cotton, linen, hemp or nettle (ramie). Yet more are manufactured synthetic fibres such as viscose and rayon which are made from wood pulp, milk protein, soya or seaweed. Re-cycled fibres are made from plastic bottles, re-used wool or denim.

There is information to get new spinners started but also to improve the skills of those with some experience. The craft is there to be enjoyed so if in doubt, try it; there is no 'one right way' and if you find something that works better for you than my methods, do it and enjoy.

a brief history of spinning

Spinning has been with us since people first became farmers and maybe longer. The first time someone twisted grasses together to make a piece of rope they were spinning.

People spun whatever was available in their local area and still do to some extent. For instance, if you lived in a country where wild cotton grew you spun cotton. If you raised animals you spun their hair or fibre. Coarse animal hair such as that from horses, goats and cattle was used to make not only ropes and bridles but industrial belts for machinery. 'Belting yarn' made from horse hair is still produced in China and some Eastern European countries but many Western countries now use metal 'yarn' for belting.

So although when we think of spinning we usually think of knitwear, everything from fine lace underwear to anchor rope, blankets and carpets depends on spun yarn.

I have a bridle which was spun and woven from horse hair in Bhutan and it is as strong as leather. I was once demonstrating flax spinning at a festival to celebrate the poet Robert Burns when one of the display tent guy ropes gave way. It was no problem to spin another, much to the amazement of the organisers who had assured me there was no point 'because a guy rope needs to be strong, dear'.

home workers

In the past, people in rural areas earned part of their living as spinners or wool carders working from home. Fibre was delivered and the spun yarn collected by cart. Not everyone spun wool though and in Scotland, Ireland and many other parts of the world flax (or linen) was spun and woven into cloth for fine garments, table wear and bed linen. There were bleaching fields in many communities where woven linen cloth was laid out in the sun to whiten.

When we opened a spinning and weaving studio in 1994 it was still possible to get flax 'stricks' – combed hanks of unbleached flax fibres – direct from Ireland, where it was both grown and prepared.

hand spindles came first

Hand spindles came into being a long time before spinning wheels were invented and go back thousands of years. Spindle whorls are one of the commonest finds on archaeological digs.

Spindles are still used in many parts of the world despite the perception by many of us that spinning wheels are quicker. Anyone can make a hand spindle and the whorl (or disc that makes it spin) does not necessarily have to be round – it can even be made from crossed sticks. To make all of your own clothes you need nothing more than a sheep or other source of fibre, five sticks and a lot of time. With these sticks you can make both a spindle to spin the yarn and a loom and shuttle to weave cloth. There is something very powerful about knowing you have the skills to do it.

the Spinning Jenny

The advent of the Spinning Jenny was the end of the home working industry in many countries. People now had to work in factories in order to produce yarn and cloth and that, along with the automation of weaving, caused riots in many areas. Some Spinning Jennies, and the even larger spinning machines that came after them, still exist in museums such as the New Lanark mill in southern Scotland, established by Robert Maxwell. New Lanark was important due to its advanced policies of taking care of the welfare and education of its workers. The New Lanark spinning machines are still in commercial use and produce yarn for sale on a small scale.

spinning for craft and fun

Spinning, knitting and weaving as leisure activities crept up on us. Knitting made the transition from work to leisure almost seamlessly and is still a mixture of both in the Western world. Spinning became popular in the 1970s with the self-sufficiency movement and a number of books for the leisure market were written about spinning at that time. Groups and Guilds became more widespread as people began to get together and spin and there is now a worldwide network.

Spinning is gaining even more popularity along with the recent upsurge of interest in knitting, crochet and other types of craftwork and there are over 120 spinning Guilds in the UK alone. There are also many in the US, which has a strong spinning and knitting culture, and throughout the rest of the world. In addition there are countless informal spinning groups that meet just to spin and chat. There are spinning suppliers and craft workers who earn their living from spinning and a 'slow crafts' movement developing as a way of helping people to recover from stressful working lives.

In times of recession spinning and knitting, along with other crafts, become even more popular. People not only want to save money but also want to get back to basics and do things that have intrinsic value with roots in the past.

why spin your own yarns?

I saw someone spinning...

People want to learn to spin for a variety of reasons and some may resonate with you. Whatever the reason that desire is usually sparked off by seeing someone spinning at a local fete, flower show or other event. That is why we spinners love to spin in public – it is how we all got the bug and we want to pass it on! I am no exception and went home in a state of great excitement the first time I saw a spinner. I just had to learn.

I want a relaxing but useful hobby

Spinning is not a demanding or complicated hobby once you know the basics. It is easy to spin and talk at the same time and it is a great way to relax. If on the other hand you do want a greater challenge, complex or more precise yarns demand a lot of concentration.

Spinning does not require good eyesight unless you want to spin very fine or fancy yarns and sometimes people turn to it because hobbies like embroidery have become too much for their eyes. In fact I once had a customer who taught a group of blind Girl Guides to spin.

I want to meet like-minded people

There are spinning and weaving Guilds all over the world. Spinners are a friendly lot and welcome beginners. There are usually people within a Guild who teach spinning and Guilds often organise workshops – it is a great way to meet people as well as improve your spinning. Have a look at the Association of Guilds of Weavers, Spinners and Dyers' website, see *resources* page 219, to find Guilds in the UK. An Internet search will provide information about Guilds in other countries. Informal groups can be harder to find. Your most local Guild will probably know about other groups in their area and there will be members in common so even if a Guild is some distance away it can be worth getting in touch.

Once you can spin, it is possible to go almost anywhere in the world and make contact with like-minded people.

I want to spin yarns for knitting or other hobbies

If you already knit, crochet, embroider or weave, producing your own yarns can add interest and satisfaction to existing hobbies. Learning to spin rekindled my own interest in knitting and crochet. Having become bored with commercial yarns, the knitting had ground to a halt but this has never happened with hand-dyed and handspun yarns. It is an added bonus that the very yarns which are quickest and easiest to spin are often the most expensive to buy – a multicoloured, thick, singles yarn with bits in it like some of the yarns produced by Noro for example.

I want to save money by spinning my own yarns

Saving money on expensive knitting yarn is another great reason to learn to spin. Whether it will save you money may well depend on what you spin. If you find you love to spin silk, it will cost more than cheap, acrylic yarn. There is no comparison between the two though and it will most certainly be cheaper to spin your own silk than to buy ready-spun silk, baby camel or other luxury yarns. It does take some self discipline to stay frugal as there are so many wonderful fibres, spinning wheels and hand spindles to be had. Then, of course, you may want to learn to weave and there are lots more wonderful things you can buy for weaving.

I want to spin the fibre from my animals

Many people start with animals such as sheep, Alpacas or an angora rabbit and then decide later on to spin the fibre. They may even have a Samoyed dog or a fluffy cat and want to spin the fur. The reverse also happens – people start out as spinners and then progress to keeping fibre animals.

Sheep can be quite labour intensive according to some of my smallholder friends and I have never gone down the road of keeping larger fibre animals. Looking after them would reduce the time available for spinning and knitting. I have kept an angora rabbit though.

I did try rearing silk worms which was interesting but unsuccessful. A friend who succeeded spent a lot of time picking birch and privet to keep her voracious caterpillars fed. She provided nice egg boxes for them to spin the cocoons in but they ended up pupating all over the house. It is a great thing to try and kids love it but I was a little relieved that mine did not survive and turn into a major feeding project.

If you are a smallholder one of the side benefits of spinning is getting to know other spinners who may want to buy some of your fleeces or at least give them a good home.

fig 1: Alpacas are inquisitive animals

I have access to lots of free fibre

I once spun 5 bin bags full of Qiviut, or musk ox for an Arctic scientist who had collected it whilst working in the frozen North. Most spinners will know it as an incredibly expensive fibre that they buy in tiny quantities – but I always picture it in bin bags cluttering up my living room. The scientist never learned to spin although having access to that much fibre would have been a great reason to do so. Other people have learned, however, when someone has given them fleece or even dog fur and they didn't want it to go to waste.

I want to make things that are environmentally friendly

It is satisfying to create your own yarns and garments from scratch. It speaks to something deep within us when we make things from the very beginning – starting with an animal and ending up with a sweater.

It is not just because people want to be self sufficient that they make their own clothes from start to finish though. In his book *Through the Eye of a Needle* John-Paul Flintoff talks about the ethical issues present in the textile industry, even for products made in America. One way to ensure at least some of your clothes are as environmentally friendly as possible is to make them yourself with yarn spun from local fibre that can be traced from start to finish.

A fleece for spinning can usually be sourced from a local farmer for a small sum, or even free especially if it is a coloured one that has no real commercial value. Even organic fleece can be had for a good price if you have a local organic sheep farmer. Alpaca, angora and mohair are also often available locally.

The British Wool Marketing Board, see *resources* page 219, publishes an annual price list for different kinds of fleeces and can supply them direct to spinners. Their price list is also a useful tool when approaching a farmer direct about purchasing some fleece.

equipment: hand spindle or spinning wheel?

hand spindles

Hand spindles are a great way to start spinning without having to spend much money. A spindle can even be made out of a few sticks from the garden tied together with string, see page 35 for different ways to make your own spindle.

Lots of spinners continue to use a spindle whether or not they get a spinning wheel and there is a whole sub-culture of spindling enthusiasts who love them because they are simple, portable and effective spinning tools in their own right.

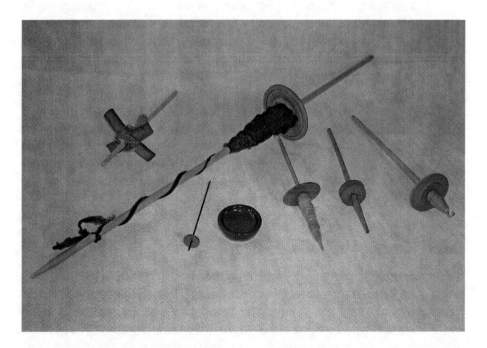

fig 2: left to right, Turkish spindle, Navajo, tahkli and support bowl, Akha, Peruvian bottom whorl spindle and high top spindle

A proficient spindle spinner (or spindler) can produce a lot of yarn. Firstly, a spindle is portable so it can be tucked into a handbag or rucksack and used at times when it would be impossible to take a spinning wheel along. Secondly, you can keep on spinning whilst wandering about and talking to friends. Wheel spinners have to stop what they are doing and get up to chat. As spinners often attend spinning groups and gatherings this is handy. I usually have a spindle with me and spin at the bus stop, in cafés and craft fairs, whilst camping and visiting friends. It is well accepted socially and seen as interesting rather than rude. As with knitting, it is a great ice breaker and a way to meet fellow knitters and spinners.

The spindle spinner Ed Franquemont from Vermont in Canada came to Scotland a number of years ago. He taught a week long course on Andean braiding and Peruvian spindle spinning which I was privileged to attend. Ed was also an anthropologist and had spent a great deal of time in Peru. At one point he and some colleagues got together and raised money to buy spinning wheels for Peruvian villagers, thinking it would make life easier for them. When they returned to the area a year later, the villagers were back to using spindles. The reason for this Ed described as *'slower by the hour, faster by the week'*. In other words, you cannot do other things whilst using a spinning wheel and are stuck at home on your own. The spinners produced less yarn and were more isolated. And the Peruvians had hand-made bottom whorl spindles – they did not even use the faster 'high top' spindles, which are commonly used in the UK and America these days.

Experience shows that this is exactly right. Taking a hand spindle away on holiday or to a spinning group means getting a whole lot more yarn spun than you would on a spinning wheel. High tops are a particular kind of spindle which are fast to spin on and a proficient spindler with a high top can produce as much yarn as an average wheel spinner.

three kinds of spindle

A spindle consists of a **shaft** or stick usually about 20-40cm (8-16in) long which goes through the centre of a disc or **whorl**. The whorl keeps it spinning for longer and gives it balance. The whorl can also be square or even made from sticks and can be either at the top or the bottom of the spindle, or sometimes even in the middle. The spinner twirls the shaft and this spins the fibre into yarn. The newly spun yarn is then wound onto the spindle by hand.

The larger the circumference of the whorl the longer and slower the spindle spins. This helps the learning process by preventing the spindle from unwinding again without you noticing. Although it is good to have a whorl with a large circumference the spindle must not be too heavy or it will be hard to use and will get even heavier once it is full of yarn.

There are three kinds of spindle to consider as a beginner and all serve well in the longer term too. These are the high top spindle - my personal favourite, the bottom whorl spindle and the Turkish spindle.

I would recommend buying a high top spindle, with a whorl about 7.5cm (3in) across and a shaft about 20-30cm (8-12in) long. It is important to have a shaft at least 20cm (8in) long as there will otherwise not be enough room for your hand to spin the spindle when there is yarn on it. There are more detailed instructions on how to use a high top spindle from page 73.

A good weight for a spindle is 20-40g (1-2oz) – a bit more if it is a Turkish spindle.

high top spindles

High tops are one of the easiest and most productive spindles to use.

A high top spindle means you can 'roll' the spindle against your thigh and can 'kick' it by holding it between your feet and drawing one foot back against the other. This gives more speed and means you can spin longer lengths of yarn at a time before winding it onto the spindle. This will not make a lot of sense right now, but will be explained later.

Thigh rolling and kicking make spindling easier and faster. Using these techniques it is possible to produce almost as much yarn on a spindle as you can on a spinning wheel, which is why high top spindles have become more popular than bottom whorl spindles in many countries.

fig 3: high top spindle – note the yarn hook at the top.

you only need one spindle

It is only necessary to buy one spindle. If, having bought a high top, you decide you want a bottom whorl spindle after all, convert the high top by turning it upside down. Put a notch in the end of the shaft that is farthest away from the whorl to hold the yarn. The spindle can then be used as either a high top or a bottom whorl spindle.

A notch is better than a hook, which could get in the way when the spindle is used as a high top again. A bottom whorl can similarly be converted to a high top spindle, by screwing a small hook into the very bottom of the shaft and then turning the spindle the other way up. Turkish spindles can be converted in the same way.

bottom whorl spindles

Most people find bottom whorl spindles slower than high tops. It takes longer to wind the yarn onto the spindle and it is not possible to 'kick' the spindle, a technique that really speeds things up.

fig 4 bottom whorl spindle – the yarn notch is top left of the photo

You can actually use the other high speed technique, 'thigh rolling' on a bottom whorl spindle as long as the yarn is spiralled around the shaft when it is wound onto the spindle. It is harder though and some people struggle to wind the yarn on in this way. If you are already a bottom spindle spinner this may be useful information. If not, ignore it and learn on a high top.

Turkish spindles

Turkish spindles are a different version of the bottom whorl spindle. Instead of a round disc (or whorl) they have two flat pieces of wood in a cross shape. These have a hole in the middle and the shaft of the spindle goes through this hole. One advantage is that they spin more slowly and keep going for longer and as a result they are relatively easy to learn on.

The yarn is wound around the cross pieces in a diagonal fashion or in a two-up-one-down formation. In theory the cross pieces can then be pulled out leaving a ball of yarn. I say in theory because the yarn may become tangled if the cross pieces don't come out easily so at first it may be better to wind the yarn off by hand in the usual way.

fig 5: Turkish spindle – the yarn is wound around the cross pieces after it is spun. The yarn notch is top left of the picture.

other kinds of spindles

These are not really for a beginner and are best ignored when starting out. With the exception of the Navajo spindle, none of them is necessary – you can do pretty much any type of spinning on one of the three spindles described above. Some people like to have different spindles just for fun, and collect them or use them for different purposes, but one is all you really need.

support spindles

Spindles that rest on the floor or in a dish or bowl are called *support spindles* and come in all sizes. The Navajo spindle is probably the largest example of this kind of spindle and the Tahkli is one of the smallest.

Any spindle can be used as a support spindle simply by resting the end of it on the floor, a table, your thigh or in a bowl whilst spinning. So there is really no need to buy a special support spindle – with the exception of the Navajo spindle, which is useful as it is specially designed for spinning thicker yarns in large quantities.

When spinning very fine yarn, support is especially important if the spindle is heavy, as it prevents the weight of the spindle from breaking the yarn. An excellent support bowl for any spindle can be made out of an empty drinks can. Simply turn the can upside down and use the bowl-shaped bottom of the can wedged between the knees as a support bowl. It can even be shaped for greater comfort by squeezing it into the perfect shape to fit between the knees.

Navajo spindles

Navajo spindles are used to spin very thick yarn, such as that used for Navajo rugs. Because they are much larger than other spindles, more of the thick yarn fits onto the spindle and it is possible to spin 500g (1lb) of thick yarn in one go on a Navajo spindle. They are ideal for spinning low-twist singles knitting yarns like Lopi.

These spindles were originally used by Navajo Indians to spin yarns for rugs, blankets and patterned knitwear and are still in use in many areas, including Mexico. There are a number of cultural initiatives in South America to promote and support traditional Navajo spinning, weaving and knitting with its distinctive stylised patterns of birds, animals and zigzags.

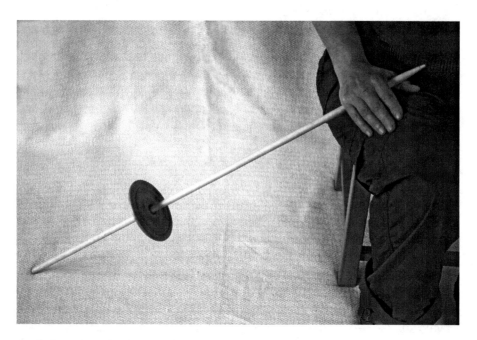

fig 6: Navajo spindle showing spinning position

To spin with a Navajo spindle, sit down and rest the tip of the spindle on the floor. The other end of the shaft rests on the outer thigh, making this the largest support spindle in general use. The floor supports the weight of the spindle and the yarn wound onto it.

The shaft of the spindle is twirled against the thigh in order to spin and then hooked back to the starting position between thumb and forefinger whilst still in motion.

The length of the shaft and the position of the whorl on the shaft will determine the height you need to sit at, so try this out and make sure you buy one suitable for someone sitting in a chair; unless you want to sit on a cushion on the floor in true Navajo style.

The yarn is initially soft spun from a pre-drafted roving with the roving coming off the tip of the spindle shaft as you spin. It is then re-spun to insert more twist.

Tahkli

Tahklis are small brass support spindles used for spinning fine yarn from shorter fibres – i.e. less than 5cm (2in) long. They are traditionally used along with a pretty pottery or wooden support bowl. Fine yarn can be spun on any spindle that is not too heavy though so a Tahkli – which is actually quite heavy – is not really necessary. Rest your existing spindle on the floor or a table, in the wrong end of an empty drinks can as described on page 31 or as a last resort in a nice bowl that you have to buy.

fig 7: Tahkli spindle with support bowl

See the section on spinning fine yarns on a spindle, page 195, for more information. Tahklis are a slow way to spin short fibres and most people who have them do not use them often.

Akha

These spindles are used by the Akha tribes of Thailand to spin cotton.

They are very light and have a whorl near the centre of the shaft rather than at the end. Spinning on an Akha spindle is a two-stage process, a bit like the larger Navajo spindle. To begin with, the spinner twists the spindle by hand whilst pulling on the fibre at the same time. This makes a loosely spun roving.

The fibre is then spun for a second time in the usual way, by suspending the spindle from the yarn that has already been spun and twirling it. Akha women throw the spindle off the thigh in much the same way as we Westerners use a high top spindle.

fig 8: Akha spindle used for spinning cotton

This two-stage process is used in order to ensure that the yarn is evenly drafted and has enough twist. It is a useful technique and a version of it can be used with other spindles, by simply spinning lightly in the normal way and then spinning the yarn a second time to insert more twist.

The Akha spindle is best for short fibres such as cotton and cashmere. The spindle can spin at great speed and is a much more effective tool than the Tahkli.

how to make a spindle

Before you spend any money, try making your own low-impact spindle. You will probably want to buy a more sophisticated spindle or a spinning wheel if you get keen but making your own means you can try spinning for the first time without having to spend money. Some people continue to use home-made spindles as a conscious choice and get lots of satisfaction from doing so.

I am including a number of ideas for making spindles – some of them are more makeshift than others. All kinds of things can be used to make a spindle and you are bound to think of some ideas of your own.

All of these spindles can be made as either a top whorl or bottom whorl spindle, except the one made from a potato, which is probably better as a bottom whorl spindle.

To make a spindle, put a stick (or shaft) right through the centre of a disc, or whorl as it is called, so that it sticks out the other end by 2.5-5cm (1-2in).

Remember it is then flexible and can be either a top or bottom whorl spindle, depending on whether you put a hook in the top or the bottom of the shaft. And of course if you put a hook in the bottom and a notch in the top, it can be used either way up in just the same way as spindles that you buy.

Here are some more detailed instructions on how to make different types of spindles.

the stick spindle
(with thanks to Debbie Zawinski)

This is the ultimate low-impact spindle. It makes a bottom whorl spindle but the design can be adapted to make it a top whorl. Debbie, who loves to travel, worked out how to make these when she was away and did not have a spindle with her.

You can simply pick up sticks from the garden or park and cut them to size with a penknife. One long stick is used for the shaft and 4 shorter ones go around it as a 'whorl'.

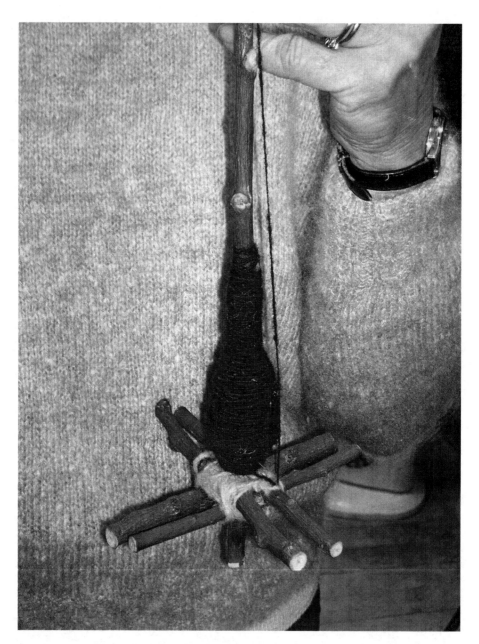

fig 9: Debbie's home-made stick spindle

The whorl is made from two pairs of crossed sticks. The spindle shaft goes between the pairs of crossed sticks and they are tied together as in fig 9. First place one stick on either side of the spindle shaft and tie them together at each side of the shaft to hold them roughly in place.

Repeat with the second pair of sticks, but make sure you tie them at right angles to the first ones.

If you are good at knots, now tie all the sticks securely to the shaft with string using a square lashing. Otherwise, just go under and over pairs of sticks in turn, keeping it really firm, then tie the ends off. The ends of the sticks can be trimmed with secateurs if necessary.

If you use freshly cut sticks, they will shrink over time and the string will become loose. Simply re-tie the sticks in place more tightly with fresh string if this happens.

The spindle will get considerably lighter as the sticks dry out; if this becomes a problem, extra weight can be added by sticking Blu-Tack, plasticene or anything else that you have to hand onto the cross sticks.

from an old CD

CDs make great spindles and it is satisfying to use something that would otherwise be thrown away. Children enjoy making them and a make-and-use-a-spindle project is a good classroom or party topic.

fig 10: left to right; a home-made CD spindle and a spindle made from a slice of potato and a pencil

Because CDs make a relatively large spindle whorl, the spindle spins slowly making this a good beginner's spindle. It can be made as a top or bottom whorl spindle. The only tricky thing is getting the spindle shaft to fit tightly into the centre of the CD as the hole is often too big for the stick.

Use a rubber washer in the centre of the CD to make it the right size. Once you have a source of washers it is easy. If you cannot find a washer, some thick rubber bands can be wound around the shaft or a bit of plastic pipe can be slid up the shaft and glued into place. Even a blob of Blu-Tack works as a less permanent solution. The Blu-Tack can be re-positioned every so often if necessary.

Another solution is to use a smooth stick which is a little bit big to fit in the hole then shave it until it fits in the hole tightly. You do not need to shave the whole stick only one end up as far as the whorl.

from a potato and a pencil

Use a small, light potato of a reasonably even shape, or a slice from a larger potato and just spear the potato with the pencil. Voila – a spindle, see fig 10.

This does not make the greatest spindle in the world, but it is instant, easy to do and is of course how I learned. A pencil can be used as a shaft for any spindle. The yarn can be looped around the pencil to hold it onto the spindle. To do this make a loop and turn it over so that the end is coming from underneath. Put the loop over the top of the spindle. The fact that the end is underneath means it does not come undone. Alternatively, cut a notch in the pencil.

from a square piece of wood and a stick

The whorl or round disc on the spindle does not actually need to be round at all. A square one works just as well. First, find the exact centre. To find the centre of a square draw 2 diagonal lines from corner to corner so they meet in the middle. If you are accurate, and the wood is truly square, the centre is where they meet. This is where you drill a hole to put the shaft through.

To find the centre of a circle, draw around it on a piece of paper. Cut the circle out and fold it in half. Then fold it in half again so that it is quartered. If you do this accurately the point where the lines cross is the centre. Lay this carefully on top of the whorl and stick a pin through to mark the centre. Then drill the hole at that point.

just a reminder: a high top is a very good choice...

Just to re-cap: If you want to buy a spindle, get a high top with a whorl of about 7.5cm (3in) across, a shaft 20-30 cm (12-18in) long, weighing no more than 40g. And by all means have a go with the potato and pencil or CD spindle before you buy one.

Buy from a reputable supplier, see the suppliers list in *resources*, page 219, give them the specifications above and explain that you are a beginner. Above all do not be tempted to spend a lot of money thinking you will get a better spindle. It may look fancy but will spin just the same and many cheaper spindles look just as lovely anyway.

If you want to continue using a stick spindle or other home-made spindle, make a high top version and experiment to get the weight right.

spinning wheels

Some people have always wanted a spinning wheel. If that is the case, you might as well learn on a wheel from the start unless cost is a major consideration. Spindle spinning can help to some extent, but the techniques are different and spindling is not a prerequisite for wheel spinning.

fig 11: Ashford Traditional spinning wheel with lazy kate

how a spinning wheel works

It is not necessary to know all about spinning wheels in order to be able to spin. So if it seems bewildering right now, just miss this bit out. Once you can spin it will be obvious anyway. These details are included here because it may be useful information to have when you are buying a wheel.

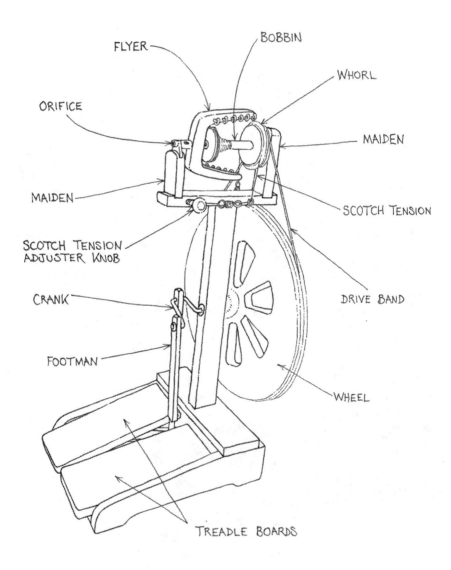

fig 12: the parts of a spinning wheel

A spinning wheel does essentially the same thing as a hand spindle in that it twists the fibre which turns it into yarn. The spinner still drafts (or pulls out) the fibre, but the wheel does the twisting and winds the yarn onto the bobbin instead of it being wound on by hand as it is on a spindle.

When the spinner moves their hand forwards (towards the flyer), it releases the tension on the yarn. The bobbin then slows down but the flyer keeps moving at the same speed. The flyer then rotates around the bobbin and this is what winds the yarn on. Once you try rotating the flyer on a spinning wheel by hand whilst holding the bobbin still you will see this happening and it will all make sense.

Most wheels are powered by treadling with your feet – some use one foot (single treadle) and some use two feet on separate treadles (double treadle). There are a few such as charkhas - the small spinning wheels made famous in India by Ghandi – and great wheels that are rotated by hand.

In this book I will talk mainly about *treadle* spinning wheels. Some information about charkhas and great wheels is included though and they are great fun to use.

Although spinning wheels can look different to each other, their essential parts are similar. There is an actual *wheel* which can vary in size. There is a *treadle board* which the spinner treadles in order to turn the wheel. This is joined to the wheel by a piece of wood called the *footman,* at the top of which is a bent bit of metal called the *crank.* This crank goes through the centre of the wheel so that the wheel turns when you treadle.

Adjacent to the wheel is the *flyer assembly*. This consists of uprights called *maidens* which have bearings on them to hold the *flyer* itself. The flyer is normally U-shaped and has hooks or a sliding metal loop to guide the newly spun yarn onto a *bobbin.* The bobbin sits on a spindle in the middle of the flyer. The whole bobbin, flyer and maidens assembly is called the *mother of all*. Wonderful names, huh?

A *drive band* joins the wheel and the flyer assembly in a loop, a bit like the chain on a bicycle. This band is often just a piece of string but can be stretchy plastic.

There are three ways for the drive band and tension to work – Scotch tension, double drive and bobbin lead. These are explored in the *how to spin on a spinning wheel* chapter, see page 93.

orifice size

The standard orifice on most wheels works for most yarn so this is not something you need to worry about if buying a recognised brand. This is one reason to avoid antique wheels which often have a small orifice – and that will really stop you learning and reduce the range of what you can spin on the wheel.

The S10/S15 series of Louet wheels have a larger orifice size which is useful (but not essential) when learning or spinning thick or fancy yarns. Some Louet wheels have a removable centre to the orifice which provides different sizes.

Wheels such as the Majacraft have a hook or metal loop instead of an orifice and these will also cope easily with thicker yarns.

A small orifice is really only an advantage when spinning very fine yarns and the lace flyers described in the following section, see page 47, have smaller orifice sizes for that reason.

accessories

There are a few necessary accessories to go with a spinning wheel.

lazy kate

A lazy kate holds the bobbins full of spun singles yarn when you are plying. You 'ply' two strands of singles yarn by twisting or plying them together in the opposite direction from which they were spun. A lazy kate is essential for this and usually comes with the spinning wheel if you buy it new. Some lazy kates are free standing and some are actually on the spinning wheel. You can make one and how to do this is explained on page 115. There are various kinds of lazy kate; the type shown in fig 13 holds three bobbins in line. Others are pictured in the *plying* chapter, see page 115, including some home-made ones which cost nothing.

fig 13 a lazy kate

niddy noddy

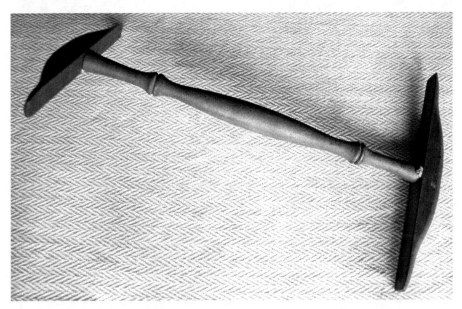

fig 14: a niddy noddy is useful and inexpensive

A niddy noddy enables you to wind the yarn off the bobbin into a skein, ready for washing or dyeing. It does not usually come with the wheel but they are inexpensive. The yarn can be wound around a large book or a picture frame if you do not have one. Life is so much easier if you do have one that they are worth buying. The Ashford ones work particularly well because the sloped arms make it easy to get the yarn off again. Beware of any that have straight arms as the yarn gets tighter as you wind and it can be hard to remove it.

spare bobbins

At least three bobbins are necessary so that you can spin two bobbins of singles yarn and then ply them onto a third one. New wheels come with three bobbins but if you buy one second-hand there might only be one. Extra bobbins can be bought from spinning suppliers. If the end of any second-hand bobbins is broken, this can be fixed with glue. (The kind that comes in two tubes and sets very hard is best.) Then sand off any rough edges on the bobbins but do not sand the grooves at the ends of the bobbins or the central core. Just smooth any bits that yarn could catch on.

fig 15: bobbins vary from wheel to wheel; pictured from left to right are Timbertops, Majacraft standard bobbin, Majacraft jumbo bobbin and Ashford standard bobbin

high speed flyers

High speed flyers are available for many wheels. As a beginner you will not need one, but if you want to spin very fine yarns or want extra speed later on they are a good buy. On Louet wheels the whorls which determine the speed are on the end of the bobbin rather than the flyer. You therefore need to buy high speed bobbins instead of a high speed flyer for these wheels.

fig 16: Majacraft jumbo and standard flyers and bobbins

jumbo flyers

Jumbo flyers are for spinning very thick yarn such as rug yarn, or for fancy yarns which have texture and loops that would get caught on a standard flyer. You can manage most yarns on a standard flyer and would not often use a jumbo flyer, so like the lace flyer it is not something you need, but rather something you may want later on.

learn to spin before you buy

One of the biggest mistakes is to assume that all spinning wheels work as well as each other. The two main factors that will govern how easily you learn to spin are the wheel you are using and whether you know other people who can spin.

It really is not possible to try out a spinning wheel if you cannot spin. Unfortunately many people buy second-hand wheels that seem like bargains but are actually only suitable as ornaments.

fig 17: classroom with some of the many modern spinning wheel designs available.

Spinning groups often have wheels that they lend or hire out to members who want to learn – both of the groups I attend have wheels available. Borrowing or hiring a wheel lets you take your time and decide which one is best for you.

If you go along to a Guild, members will have different makes and styles of wheel so it is possible to find out more about the different types. There are often second-hand wheels for sale too. Good, professionally-made wheels all do the same job but some are more portable than others, some look more traditional and others more contemporary.

It is probably a bit harder to teach yourself to spin on a wheel than on a spindle because there are more things that can go wrong. If you do get stuck, seek the advice of local spinners or book a day's course. Often the things that self-taught spinners get stuck on are very simple to sort out – if only you know what to look for.

Just one point here though – it is not polite to go along to a spinning group and expect members to spend all day teaching you to spin free of charge. They have come along to do their own spinning and see friends. Whilst they will more than likely be delighted to help you out and give tips do not expect a full day's spinning lesson. If you need more focused help, ask who does classes and workshops in the area.

get a modern wheel and buy from an established maker

Get a modern spinning wheel that is designed and made by a recognised manufacturer. This can include second-hand wheels as some modern makers have been producing wheels for many years.

There are a number of good manufacturers and pretty much any of their wheels will spin well and last almost indefinitely and information is included about some of them.

I have not mentioned them all, but the list is a good selection and they are available in a number of countries through local spinning supply shops and specialist mail order companies. The timber used varies from wheel to wheel and can change as new styles are introduced so a list of materials used is not included. It is best to check with the supplier if you are buying a new wheel. All of the manufacturers I mention use wood from reputable sources. On some the actual wheel is made from fibre board, while some include laminates.

Ashford

Made in New Zealand these are probably the commonest wheels in use worldwide. They are versatile and offer a range of designs including folding options. Most of the wheels are available with either single or double treadle and Ashford sell a conversion kit which can change a single treadle wheel to a double which is very handy if you buy an older, second-hand one.

The Ashford Traditional can often be picked up second-hand. The wheels have a good range of accessories available. Older wheels can easily be upgraded with a new, high-speed flyer. People sometimes start out with an Ashford Traditional wheel then change it for one that is more portable, which is why Ashford Traditionals are often available second-hand and relatively cheaply.

fig 18: Ashford Traveller spinning wheel

Louet

Made in Holland most of these wheels have a large orifice which can be handy when learning. Some Louets have an orifice with a removable centre part, giving a choice of two different orifice sizes. These wheels are robust and well engineered. The Louet S10 can often be bought second-hand but

fig 19: Louet Victoria spinning wheel.

do not be tempted to buy one unseen from an online auction site. They are robust wheels and there is little that cannot be fixed but I know someone who bought one unseen only to find that the bobbin was glued to the shaft of the flyer as it had been used for display purposes.

Louet do a range of versatile wheels including some that fold. They also do a skeinwinder which attaches to the top of some of the wheels and is very handy indeed. High speed bobbins are available to obtain a wider range of ratios and these are a good addition to older wheels.

Timbertops

Made in the UK these are hand-made wheels of the most exquisite kind, made from oak. They come in a range of styles including some unusual older ones. I have a Timbertops chair wheel which is many years old. It is my all-time favourite spinning wheel though possibly not the one I would have chosen to learn on. These wheels are not cheap or the most portable. There are double and single treadle models available and a number of different designs.

The chair wheel is surprisingly portable though. Its square shape means you can lay it on its back and put other stuff inside the middle of it in the boot or back seat of a car. No good if you want to get four spinners and four wheels in a car though, you need a folding wheel like the Ashford Joy or Majacraft Little Gem for that.

Lendrum

Made in Canada these are double treadle wheels that fold up. The wheel is tilted towards you, which some people find helpful, and they are easy to fold. Many owners recommend them and find them versatile and easy to use.

Majacraft

Made in New Zealand the Majacraft Little Gem is a lovely portable wheel. It is not quite as easy to fold as the Ashford Joy, but it is still pretty easy especially once you get used to it. The wheel is in fact so compact that there is no need to fold it up for most journeys. One advantage over the Ashford Joy is that it has a wider range of ratios which suits me because I like to spin fast.

fig 20: Timbertops chair wheel

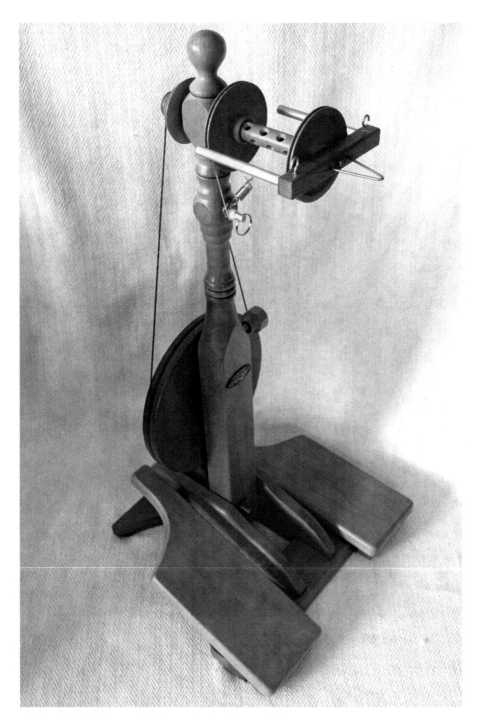

fig 21: Majacraft Little Gem folding wheel

Another advantage is that Majacraft wheels have a wire hoop instead of an orifice on the flyer. This means that you can easily spin textured or thick yarns and do not need a threader hook to get the yarn through the orifice. There is a jumbo flyer available which is easy to swap over without any adaptation. Majacraft supply a great skeinwinder which can either be free standing or attached to the wheel. You cannot have the bobbin and skeinwinder on the wheel at the same time unfortunately, which you can with the Louet wheel.

Majacraft also make other wheels which are larger and consequently heavier.

Schact

Made in the US the Schact, like the other wheels mentioned, has its enthusiasts. It is expensive and a beautiful piece of engineering. The thing that puts me off is that changing the bobbin is a fiddle and involves an extra stage, as opposed to the Ashfords where you just 'unclick' a bearing, or the Majacraft or Timbertops where you unscrew one end of the flyer. Louets are the easiest of the lot – you just lift the bobbin out. Schacht wheels are also heavy and quite large. Schact make a folding wheel called the Sidekick which is unusual in that the wheel is edge on to the spinner rather than side on. It then has a treadle board either side of the wheel. Not the best choice if you wear long skirts.

buy a wheel to suit your lifestyle

As you will have gathered by now, spinning tends to be a social activity. After a while, you may therefore need a wheel that can easily be taken to classes, workshops, spinning demonstrations and group gatherings.

Think about the size of your car, as well as the size of your living room when choosing a wheel. If you use public transport or are likely to share a car with other spinners, choose a wheel that is lightweight and folds into a nifty carry bag, such as the Ashford Joy or Majacraft Little Gem.

I have even put an Ashford Joy in the front bag of my Brompton folding bicycle and cycled to a spinning group complete with wheel. Obviously a hand spindle would be a more usual choice for this mode of transport but I wanted to see if it could be done.

A wheel that will not fall apart or otherwise suffer from being transported is also handy. Some have legs that push into place rather than being attached with screws, pegs or bolts. In theory they should stay put but tend not to. They loosen over time if the wood shrinks and contracts due to changes in temperature and humidity.

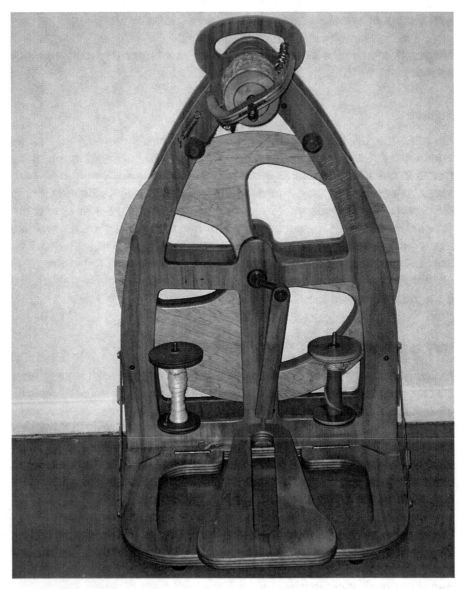

fig 22: Ashford Joy folding wheel

Folding wheels are hard to get second-hand and quite a lot more expensive than ordinary wheels. A second-hand Ashford traditional or Louet S10 or S15 is a good choice and probably the easiest to obtain. They are robust wheels unlikely to have much wrong with them and spare parts are easily available. A non-folding but compact wheel like the Ashford Traveller is also very transportable in the back seat or boot of a car. If you put a wheel on the back seat be sure to put a seat belt around it so that it does not hit you on the back of the head if someone drives into the back of you.

I have a small car and can fit two or three non-folding wheels on the back seat depending on what they are. They would not be so easy to take on public transport, especially if it was crowded and a folding wheel really is better in that case.

clean the wheel before you use it

If you have bought a second-hand wheel check it carefully because it may well have been used to spin wool in the grease – i.e. without washing it first.

It is common for people who have bought a perfectly good second-hand wheel to find they cannot get it to work properly. The two main reasons are a build up of grease in the orifice and a groove that has worn to a cutting edge on the flyer hooks.

To clean the orifice, soak a piece of paper towel in oil and then wrap it around the unsharpened end of a pencil and push it into the orifice. It will take several goes and often the grease will not come out until it has been soaked in oil. Do not be tempted to scrape the oil away as you may damage the inner surface of the orifice.

I once taught a class where someone was sure the orifice on her wheel was clean but the yarn kept breaking. She cleaned the orifice but not thoroughly as she was really not convinced it needed it. When everyone went for lunch, I had another go and gave it a real soaking. After lunch, she began spinning and a large plug of solid grease popped out. There had been hardly any space left for the yarn to get through at all, and the grease also causes friction.

Sometimes there is grease on the flyer itself where the yarn has travelled over it and this should also be removed.

Use sandpaper to smooth down rough edges on the flyer hooks. While you are at it, remove any rough edges on the bobbins and the wooden parts of the flyer. Do not sand the groove on the bobbin where the drive band or Scotch tension goes, or the band will slip.

It is fine to spin in the grease if you want to, but see the section on sorting and washing fleece first, page 134 – and clean that wheel regularly.

don't make your own – and don't buy an antique

When I teach beginners, I take a spare spinning wheel with me in case someone turns up with a 'tricky' wheel. Often this is one that even an expert would struggle to use; sometimes it will not spin at all because some vital part is missing or very slightly out of alignment.

These wheels are often of sentimental value and inheriting an antique wheel may even be the reason someone wanted to learn to spin in the first place. They may persist valiantly (I am sure I would have done the same) making little progress until they finally have a 'little go' at my suggestion on a modern, well set-up, professionally-made wheel. The usual response is 'oh this is easy!'. As a beginner you nearly always think it is you and not the wheel that is at fault – and you will usually be wrong.

Admittedly it is a bit tricky if your beloved has made you a spinning wheel and you have to go home and say 'er, actually I need to buy another wheel, this one is no good'.

Making a spinning wheel is not for the fainthearted and it is said that you need to make between four and seven of them before you get a good one.

Here's a suggestion: if you are attached to your antique or hand-made wheel learn to spin on a modern, professionally-made wheel first. Once you can spin use the other one sometimes and you will do better with it. Just don't try to learn on it. The only thing is by that time you may not want to.

If you want to spin with something home-made, use a spindle – you can produce a lot of yarn on a spindle and do not really need a wheel at all.

if you really must make your own...

Make one from an old bicycle! This actually works and a member of my Guild made one a few years ago. It was rather heavy though and that, combined with the shape, meant it was not easy to carry around.

A bicycle, of course, has bearings and a wheel so you are off to a very good start. Instructions are in the book *Spinning and Weaving at Home* by Thomas Kilbride, see *resources* page 219.

If you want to make your own wooden wheel, are a very proficient wood turner and can either spin yourself or have a spouse or close friend who can, then instructions are available from David Bryant. He is a spinning wheel maker and he and his wife are spinners and spinning wheel historians. They can also supply the metal parts for some of the wheels they sell 'patterns' for, see *resources* page 219.

Do not be tempted to buy instructions from wood turners who are not spinners. I have seen a procession of such wheels over the years and cannot think of any that were much good. Some did not work at all. It is often fine adjustments that are at fault and these are almost impossible to fix.

the charkha, the great wheel and other point-of-contact wheels

You may have seen pictures of Ghandi spinning on a charkha. He made a political statement by spinning as well as producing yarn. Most Indian cotton fibre was exported to the United Kingdom for spinning and he believed that if India became self-sufficient in cotton yarn and fabric it would hurt the UK financially and help India to gain independence.

Charkhas are quite different to the spinning wheels we are accustomed to seeing in the Western world and, instead of having an orifice, they have a **point** from which the yarn is spun. A charkha is a small, portable wheel and many of them fold up like a book, into a little box which is typically about 15cm (6in) by 25cm (10in) in size.

Charkhas are still common in many parts of the world, especially India. They are ideal for spinning fine, high-twist yarns from short fibres such as cotton, cashmere or Yak. In fact they are the instrument of choice for spinning such fibres and you will be hard pressed to find a better and quicker way to do it.

fig 23: Bosworth Book Charkha

One spinning wheel maker, Jonathan Bosworth, produces modern charkhas made from sustainably-grown Canadian maple wood. They have built-in bearings and can be used at a table rather than sitting on the floor. They are a joy to use and well worth the extra money they cost when compared to the more basic type imported from India.

Although the great wheel is much larger than a charkha it spins in a similar way; from a point rather than the yarn going through an orifice. Instead of sitting on the floor, the spinner stands side on to the wheel, which can have a circumference of up to 1.5m (5ft). The wheel is turned with one hand and the fibre pulled out ahead of the twist with the other, just like it is on the charkha.

Great wheels were commonly used in the United Kingdom at one time but are rarely seen now. Various point-of-contact wheels are still used in other parts of the world such as South America. David Bryant, see *resources* page 219, makes a modern version which has a much smaller wheel. The spinner can sit down when spinning and the wheel is easier to accommodate in a modern house. If you want to see one working, great wheels can still be seen in operation during demonstrations in some museums and restored weavers' cottages.

fig 24: spinning on a modern Book Charkha

fig 25: spinning on a Great Wheel

getting ready to spin: fibre

There is a lot more about fibre later in the book, see page 131. The aim of this section is purely to give you enough information to buy some fibre and get started.

Just about any yarn you see in the shops can be replicated on a spinning wheel. People spin everything from fine lace weight to jumbo-textured yarn.

When non-spinners think of spinning they probably think of using sheep's wool in natural colours. You can, of course, spin those and they remain a favourite with many spinners. You can also spin almost any other fibre – silk, Merino, cotton, linen, musk ox and mohair to name just a few.

There is a large range of prepared and unprepared fibre available, including wool in every colour of the rainbow and all different levels of fineness; from fine Merino for baby wear to hill fleece suitable for carpets.

Joining a Guild or group will give you access to all the fibre you need. There will be members who sell fleeces and other fibres and larger suppliers who visit with stalls. Guilds also get together with each other and have 'gatherings' with even more suppliers.

try a bit of everything

The wider the range of fibre you spin, the better your spinning will be so take advantage and dive in.

Sometimes people say things like 'I'm not ready to spin silk because I have only been spinning for a year'. Whilst it is true that silk is a slipperier fibre than wool and can be more challenging to spin in certain forms, some silk – for example silk cocoons – is easy and what's more you can't lose the end the way you can with wool. On beginners' courses, some people will be spinning certain types of silk by the afternoon. Occasionally someone only wants to spin silk and does so as a complete beginner because no one told them it was supposed to be hard.

all fibre is not equal

A friend was struggling with some bamboo fibre and asked me for help. I had taken a hank of beautiful grey bamboo fibre to our most recent spinning meeting but whereas mine had been a blissful roving of 7.5cm (3in) fibre, hers was made up of very short clumps of white shiny stuff. After carding we just about managed to spin it, but it was a fiddle and the result was mediocre. Our verdict was that it would make great stuffing for a cushion – a better solution than stiff fingers and frustration. Spinning is supposed to be fun after all.

pre-prepared fibres: a good place to start

As a beginner, it is important to start with good fibre. When I teach beginners in a class they learn to select, properly wash and card a fleece before starting to spin. If you are learning by yourself at home it is not easy to do all of this.

Using sub-standard or improperly carded fibre will prevent you from even getting started. As a beginner you will not know whether the fleece is a good one, whether it has been spoiled in the wash or whether you have carded it properly.

When learning on your own at home, start with commercially-prepared fibre. This leapfrogs you over all of the potential problems above. Once you have spun some commercially-prepared fibre, you will know whether any fibre you prepare yourself is good quality or not.

Commercially-prepared fibre comes in the form of what is called a **combed top** – this is a long length of combed fibre; or in a **carded mass** which is a big, fluffy bundle of carded fibre. It is sometimes easier to start with carded fibre as opposed to tops, – but not always – and either will do.

Pre-prepared fibres can be bought from specialist spinning suppliers. Use an established supplier rather than someone selling a bit of fibre on Ebay. I know of at least one person who was sold special luxury fibre which was totally unsuitable for a beginner but because she knew no better she thought she was no good at spinning and gave up. A good supplier will be able to advise you, so phone them up for a chat.

If, like most spinners, you get excited by fibre you will buy it because it is soft and lovely, or a gorgeous colour no matter what. Don't let me spoil the fun – we all do it, but don't try to work with the more challenging fibres until you have more skill.

As a beginner, stick to medium-staple length and medium-soft wool tops – so, not Merino and not luxury fibres as these are much harder to spin. Avoid hand-dyed wool tops at the beginning, as they vary in quality and some become matted in the dyeing process. Also avoid any blends with luxury fibres in them.

It is better to buy a small quantity, such as 100g (4oz) of several different wool tops. You will learn more and become a better spinner by spinning a variety of things rather than a kilo of the same thing. 100g (4oz) goes an awfully long way when you are spinning and it is best to start with small projects anyway.

A good selection of tops would be 100g each of: Black Welsh Mountain, Shetland, Bluefaced Leicester, Corriedale and Jacob. These are all varieties of sheep native to the United Kingdom but now found in other countries too and are excellent for knitwear. Romney is another possibility.

what to do when buying pre-prepared fibres

- ask the supplier as they will be able to give you advice about which fibres are best for a beginner. It is rare to find a supplier who is not also a spinner.
- avoid Merino at the beginning. This can be hard as it comes in lots of lovely colours but Corriedale is usually available in similar shades and is a better choice.
- if buying face-to-face ask if you can take the fibre out of the bag. Carefully pull a few fibres off it to take a look. This will give you an idea of the 'staple length' or length of the fibres. You are looking for 7.5-10cm (3-4in) length. If you think you might make a mess of the fibre by trying to do this, ask the supplier to do it for you.
- if you do succumb to a multi-coloured, hand-dyed roving (another name for a combed top), unroll it and have a look. A hand-dyed roving with a lot of white space in it will go much paler when spun – which is fine as long as that is what you want.

how to pre-draft for manageable spinning

Although pre-prepared fibres – tops or carded fibre - do not need carding, they do need a bit of attention before spinning. The fibres tend to stick together slightly after being stored and *pre-drafting* as it is called loosens them up again. It makes them easier, more enjoyable and faster to spin as well as breaking the fibre down to a manageable size. Without it tops can be a real challenge to work with and that is why some people struggle to spin them.

Pre-drafting means that you give the fibres little tugs – just enough to loosen them but not enough to actually pull the prepared top, or fibre mass, apart.

Pre-drafting reduces the amount of work your hands have to do whilst you are actually spinning. This is a big help when you are learning, but in fact all spinners should pre-draft as it makes the resultant yarn much more even and the spinning flows better.

Experienced spinners will usually *draft* the fibre some more whilst they are actually spinning. It is not necessary to draft and spin simultaneously though and all of the drafting can be done beforehand if desired.

Then, when spinning, simply feed in the fibre as you treadle the spinning wheel or twirl the spindle. This is the best way to do it as a beginner, but it is also useful for more experienced spinners when spinning very thick yarns as it is much harder to get these yarns even.

check the fibre (or staple) length

First of all, check the length of the fibre (staple length) by pulling a few fibres out of the prepared top or carded mass. You can do the same thing with a fleece.

This is important because the length of the fibre governs how far apart your hands should be when drafting, or pulling the fibre apart. If they are too close together, you will be pulling at both ends of the same fibres and will be unable to pull it apart. You might as well pull on both ends of a piece of string and expect it to come apart! Keep this staple length as a reference for when you are pre-drafting and spinning.

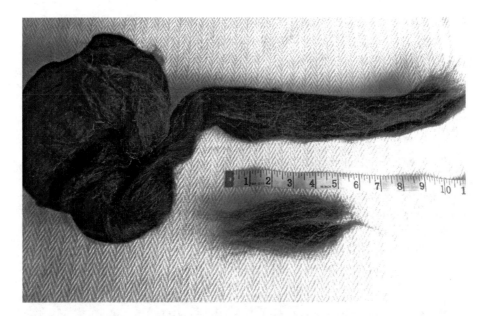

fig 26: one staple length pulled off a combed top

split the fibre before you pre-draft

fig 27: splitting the fibre prior to pre-drafting

Take a bit of fresh, good quality tops or roving and pull it apart totally so that a 60cm (2ft) long section of it comes away in your hand. If it is hard to pull it apart, then you are holding your hands too close together. Move them further apart than you think they should be and then try again. They should be at least 15-30cm (6-12in) apart most of the time. Be aware of this when you actually start to spin because a lot of people find their hands get closer together without realising.

Working with this 60cm (2ft) length, find the midpoint along its length and poke a finger through it so that you have a section about twice the width of a pencil to one side of the finger and the rest of the top to the other. Then pull it apart lengthwise from this point. You will now have a finger-wide strip of fibre to work with, which is usually known as a pencil roving, so put the rest to one side. The reason you go to the midpoint of the fibre is simply so that you then do not have so far to pull.

pull the fibre apart or it will not work!

Pulling the fibre apart sounds alarming to a beginner, whose impulse is often to try and hold it all together, but you cannot spin without pulling the fibre apart. The aim is to pull it apart by about half of its length. That way the whole roving becomes thinner without actually coming to bits. If you practise until you can do this really well, you will have mastered the major core task of the spinning process.

Get this bit wrong and the spinning will not work. It may seem like it is working for a few minutes. Then the spun yarn gets thicker and thicker until it is just one big lump. Once the fibre has some twist, it is almost impossible to draft it further. So if you find yourself pulling hard on the fibre as you spin, trying to split it by pulling sideways or other little tricks to get it to draft, you need to go back to pre-drafting and practise some more.

When you pre-draft or draft it should be easy to pull the fibres apart. You should feel them *give* as you pull. If you do not feel the give at any point when spinning or pre-drafting, go back and practise this to refresh your memory.

now pre-draft

Start pre-drafting from one end of the fibre. With your hands about 30-45cm (12-18in) apart, pull for about half of the length of the fibres. Remember you checked the length of the fibres at the start – so if they are 7.5cm (3in) long you need to pull for about 3.5cm (1.5in).

You should be drafting fibre from in front *of* your hand, not pulling it through the hand. So you need a good lot of fibre in front of that hand at all times. You cannot work on the fibre that is in your hand - it must be already in front of it.

fig 28: the pre-drafted fibre is loose and you can see daylight through it

Pause and look at the fibres. They should have loosened up and this section of the roving will be thinner, with daylight showing through.

Now let go with one hand at a time and move each hand about 10cm (4in) along the fibre so that you are pre-drafting a new section. The actual distance you move your hands will vary a little depending on the length of the fibre, but for medium length fibre this is about right.

It is important to let go completely with each hand in turn every time you move them along the fibre. This allows the fibre to re-align itself and keeps it tidy. Do not slide your hands along the fibre or pull the fibre through your hand. If you do it will become untidy with bits sticking out all over the place. These will create a fluffy mess on the spun yarn and if you are using a spinning wheel the fluff catches on the hooks and stops the yarn from winding onto the bobbin. In other words, it makes it much harder to spin.

The pre-drafted roving should look reasonably even, although this takes a bit of practise.The most important thing is to check that all of the fibres have been opened up and you have not missed any sections out. If the roving comes apart at any time, just overlap it and draft the two together.
Here's a summary:

- draft the fibres for only half of their length at a time and no more, or you will get an uneven roving
- do not drag the fibre through your hands – make sure you draft fibre that is in front of your hand
- do not slide; let go of the fibre every time you move your hands along the roving. If you get fluffy bits sticking out, you are sliding!
- if it comes apart, overlap the two lots of fibre then draft them both together

practise, practise, practise

Practise pre-drafting until you are confident that you know how to do it easily. After pre-drafting a few lengths of fibre it will seem easier.

Drafting the fibre is something that new spinners often struggle with, as the impulse is to hold the fibre together – the very opposite of what needs to happen. In order to spin you must pull the fibre apart, but not all the way; without doing this the spinning will not work.

It takes practice to get full control of the twist when you actually start spinning and, if you are working from a very long piece of fibre, it is easy to end up with twist in the unspun fibre, making it hard to draft. With a reasonably short length it is simple to hold the fibre up in the air and let it untwist.

carded fibre

To pre-draft commercially-carded fibre as opposed to combed tops, pull off a length of fibre, check the staple length and pre-draft it as above. If you are working with a carded mass of fibre rather than a carded roving, it may be more of a lump of fibre than a length that you pull off but treat it in the same way.

zigzag a carded batt

If the fibre is in an oblong **batt** produced on a drum carder, it is possible to spin it as one continuous length. Split off a length almost from one end of the batt to the other but do not detach it from the batt completely. Now turn around and split it going up in the opposite direction. Continue to zigzag like this until you have a long length. Do not worry about the corners being thicker than the rest of it. Now pre-draft and even it out but again do not worry about the corners being different to the rest – if you fiddle with it too much the batt will come apart.

fig 29: a zigzagged carded batt ready for pre-drafting

This is not the best way to proceed if you are a beginner on a spinning wheel – work with shorter lengths at first so that they do not get tangled up. It is ideal once you have got the hang of the basics because you do not have to stop so often to join on new fibre.

This is a good method however, when using a hand spindle with a wrist distaff because it means you can wind a nice long length of fibre onto the distaff. Joins on a spindle are trickier to do than with a spinning wheel so working with a longer length is helpful, even as a beginner.

how to spin on a high top spindle

Pre-drafting is the same whether you are spinning on a spindle or a spinning wheel. The principle of how yarn is spun is also the same – the spinner pulls out, or drafts, the fibre and the wheel or spindle then twists that fibre. It is the twist that transforms it from fibre to yarn.

Used correctly high top spindles are an economical, portable and easy way to make yarn. Some people learn on a spindle and then 'progress' to a spinning wheel.

Because the techniques are different, the ideal is to learn on a spindle if you want to be a spindle spinner and to learn on a wheel if you want to be a wheel spinner. If you are not sure, or the cost of a wheel is prohibitive then spindling is a great way to start.

high top spindles are easiest to learn on and the most efficient

A high top spindle has a hook in the end nearest the whorl. The yarn goes around this when you are spinning, so that the spindle is suspended from the hook by yarn that has already been spun.

The spinner twirls the spindle by flicking it with their fingers, rolling it off their thigh or by *kicking* the spindle, i.e. holding it between their feet and drawing one foot back or forwards against the other. (This is easier than it sounds and looks really cool.)

You can get the spindle to spin really fast by doing this which enables you to draft more fibre every time you spin the spindle. It also means you can ultimately learn to spin what is called *extended draw* on a high top spindle, which is a fast and enjoyable way of spinning.

practise with a piece of yarn

Now that you can draft fibre, the next stage is to get the hang of twirling or spinning the spindle. To do this, use a cone or ball of yarn. The thinner this is the better, as thinner yarns can take up more twist than thicker ones, giving you more time to practise twirling without the yarn becoming overtwisted.

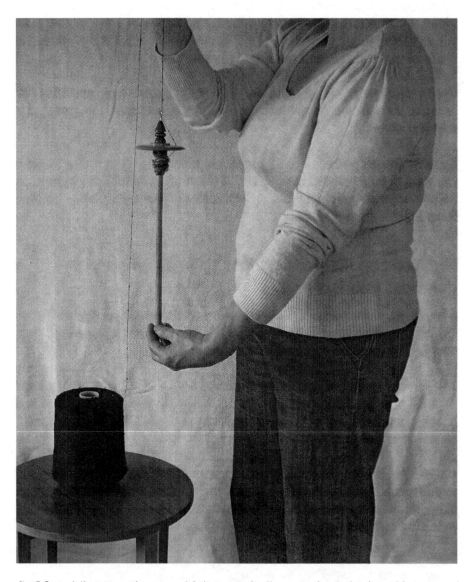

fig 30: twirling practice on a high top spindle; note how the hand is cupped under the bottom of the spindle shaft

Take the end of the yarn twice around the shaft of the spindle then tie it on. Put the cone of yarn on the floor. Take the yarn through the hook on the top of the spindle and twist it round the hook a couple of times.

Hold the yarn coming from the hook in one hand, so that the spindle is suspended by the yarn. It does not matter which hand you use, so do whatever feels comfortable. Right-handed people usually want to twirl the spindle with the right hand and left-handed people with the left one but not always.

Cup the bottom of the spindle shaft loosely in the other hand and grip the shaft between fingers and thumb. A snapping action, taking the thumb across the tips of the fingers will spin the spindle. If you snap your fingers in one direction the spindle will spin clockwise; snap them in the other direction and it will spin anticlockwise. Practise twirling so that the spindle spins clockwise until you can get it to spin well. Each time you have 'spun' one length of the yarn, take if off the hook and wind it onto the spindle so that you have a new length to practise on, just as if you had spun it for real.

The convention is to spin yarn (at this point it is called *singles* yarn) clockwise and then to ply it anticlockwise. It is spun one way and then plyed in the opposite direction in order to balance the twist and add strength.

make a wrist distaff to hold the fibre

Now that you have practised drafting fibre and twirling the spindle, there is just one more thing to do before spinning for real. That is to make a wrist distaff to hold the fibre. Without this, it is hard to manage longer lengths of fibre. Having a long length of fibre ready to spin makes spindle spinning much easier and faster, because you do not have to keep stopping to join on more fibre. As a beginner joins are tricky so having more fibre ready is very useful.

To make a wrist distaff take two broad shoe laces, two bits of thickish string, yarn or anything else that you have to hand. If you don't have thicker string, yarn or shoe laces, simply double up thinner ones or plait them to make them thicker. Use the shoe laces as they are, but if using string or yarn cut off four lengths about 45cm (18in) long – a bit longer if you are going to plait them.

Measure them to fit round your wrist so that the distaff will be easy to slip on and off but not will fall off whilst you are spinning. Tie all the strands together with an overhand knot to make a loop that goes around your wrist, see fig 31 for guidance. (An overhand knot is useful because it is a non slip knot but if you don't know how to do one any knot will do).

fig 31 wrist distaffs with and without fibre.

Tie one more knot in each of the four ends. This will help to keep the fibre from slipping off the ends of the distaff. It works best if you have the distaff on one wrist and twirl the spindle with the opposite hand so they do not get tangled up together. If you want to use your dominant hand to spin the spindle, put the distaff on the opposite wrist.

wrap the fibre around the distaff

With the distaff on your wrist, take the longish length of the pre-drafted fibre and wrap it around it. The distaff can hold a lot of fibre and should end up looking a bit like an old fashioned bee hive. Wind the fibre around so that it is tight enough to stay on but no tighter. As you spin you have to remember to unwind fibre from the distaff by hand, it will not unroll by itself.

fig 32: winding pre-drafted tops onto a wrist distaff

how to join the fibre onto the spindle

Unwind about 45cm (18in) of fibre from the distaff. Make sure there is not a surplus of fibre hanging down in a loop or this will catch into the spinning when you do not want it to.

Put the hook through the length of fibre so that it catches a narrow section of it. Begin to twist the spindle in your hand, without letting go of it. At the same time, pull the spindle backwards so that fibre is drawn out from the main mass as you twist it. This is actually a form of spinning, although it would be a slow method if used all the time. (When using the Akha spindle to spin a two-stage yarn this is the first stage of the process.) Keep the yarn under tension or it will pop off the hook and unwind itself; if it does come off, just hook it back on and twist some more.

Once you have a 45cm (18in) length of yarn, remove it from the hook and tie it around the shaft of the spindle, near the whorl. Now twist the yarn around the hook and you are ready to spin some more.

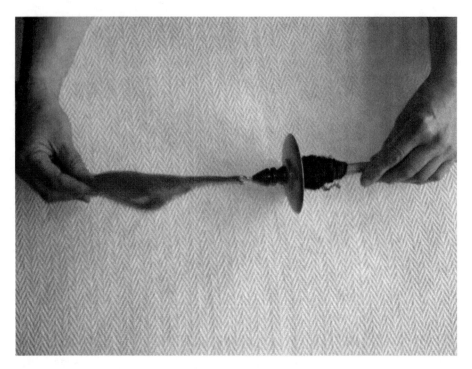

fig 33: attaching fibre to a drop spindle. The spindle will be twisted whilst pulling the fibre out in order to make enough yarn to tie around the spindle shaft

The advantage of starting off like this is that it saves you from having to do a join before you get going. It is the best way to join on fibre to start any spindle spinning whether you are a beginner or not.

Once you have spun some yarn, you can leave a good long length on the spindle, ideally with a nice, fluffy, unspun end so that you can join new fibre onto it but there is never the need to join yarn to get started using this method.

emergency measures

If you cannot get the hang of the starting technique above do not despair. Tie a length of medium thickness yarn onto the shaft of the spindle near the whorl and tie a loop in the end. Pre-draft the end of the length of fibre so that it is quite thin. Put it through the loop, double it back on itself and draft it back a little. Put the yarn around the hook of the spindle. Now twist the spindle in your hand whilst pulling it away from the fibre to draw it out as before. It can take a bit of time for the twist to go into the fibre – it will need to be thin enough for the twist to move onto it, otherwise it will twist the yarn and not the fibre. Once the fibre has some twist in it, wind it onto the spindle and then proceed as below.

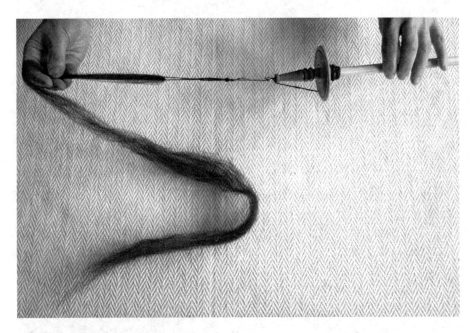

fig 34: an 'emergency' join can be used on either a spindle or a spinning wheel

Another option is to tie the yarn around a small amount of the fibre and draft it back as before. Spinning improves by doing it so it is better to tie it on and get on with spinning.

twirl, stop and draft: you don't need to do it all at the same time

twirl

Now that you have done all of the preliminary stages, the next thing is to twirl the spindle again and spin some yarn. Beginners often imagine having to do everything at once but this is not the case. Especially at the start, it really helps to spin in stages and to stop in between. This stops the yarn from becoming overtwisted and breaking and you will learn more quickly if you take your time.

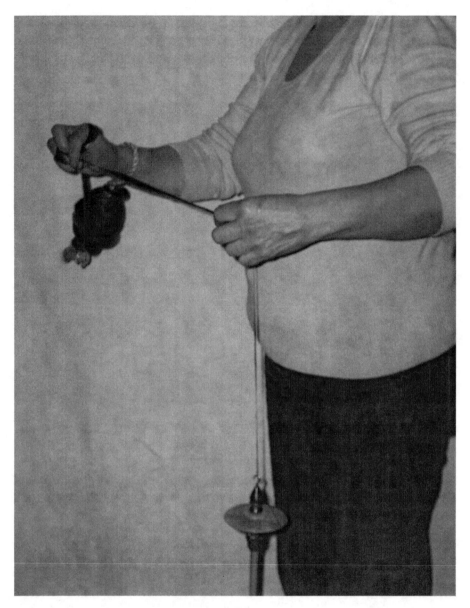

fig 35: spinning on a high top spindle

So twirl the spindle just like you did when practising with the cone of yarn. It is easiest to do this standing up. Whilst you twirl the spindle, make sure you pinch the newly-twisted yarn to stop the twist from travelling into the remaining unspun fibre. Do not attempt to draft the fibre, or let the twist go into the fibre, just build up twist in the leader yarn.

stop and let the twist through

Then stop, sit down and wedge the spindle between your knees. Now let the twist through, slowly running your hand back onto the pre-drafted fibre. The twist will turn the fibre into yarn. If the fibre is still too thick you can draft it some more before letting the twist into it. Once it has twist in it, you will not be able to draft it.

You may need to repeat this process two or three times before there is enough yarn to wind onto the spindle.

wind it on to the spindle

Now take the yarn off the hook and wind it around the shaft of the spindle, near the whorl.

Each time you wind the new yarn onto the spindle, leave about 45cm (18in) suspended from the spindle. The reason for this is that high top spindles spin fast, so you need enough yarn to deal with the twist. Otherwise the spindle will spin fast and then immediately 'bounce' back the other way and unspin again due to the yarn having too much twist in it. It may even break with an audible snap if it is severely overtwisted.

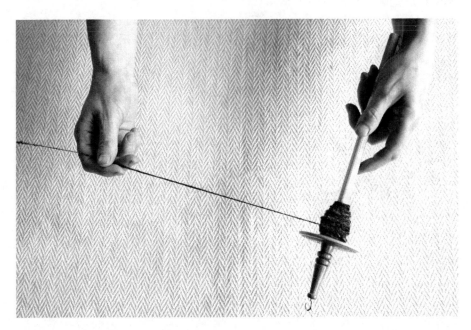

fig 36: winding yarn onto a spindle

When winding the yarn onto the spindle, aim for a beehive shape that stays compact. It should be close to the whorl and not work its way down the shaft of the spindle, otherwise it will get in the way when you twirl the spindle. The widest point should be at the centre not closest to the whorl. This means the spindle can hold more yarn without it slipping over the edge of the whorl. Do not wind the yarn on too tightly or it will work its way down the shaft. Wind it on neatly but not tight.

take stock

Pause now and take stock of what just happened. You have hopefully managed to join the fibre, hand twist that first length, twirl the spindle to spin yarn and wind it onto the spindle. Now repeat this process over and over and you are spinning.

how to join the yarn on again if it breaks

As a beginner the fibre will pull apart every so often and need joining on again. Trying to prevent this merely leads to overtwisted yarn and fibre that will not draft. So if it breaks, treat it as a learning exercise and get some practise at joining the fibre back on.

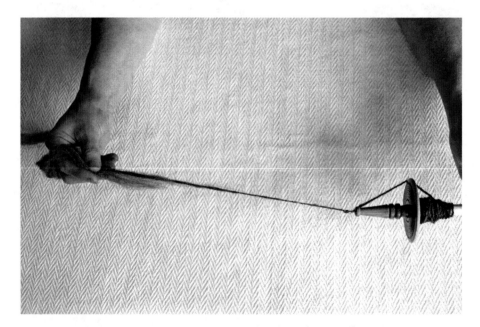

fig 37: join two fluffy ends to make a firm join

Joining can be trickier on a spindle than on a spinning wheel because the weight of the spindle is suspended from the yarn. The join can seem fine initially but as you spin and the yarn gets longer the twist spreads out, so there is less to hold the join together. The solution is to use plenty of twist when joining and to get the join wound onto the spindle as soon as possible.

Always join a fluffy end to a fluffy end. Tease the fibres out so that they are as fluffy as possible. Then build up some twist and pinch the yarn with the fingers to hold this twist back. Overlap the new and old fibre then let the twist through. Use a lot of twist and overlap the two ends by a good distance.

If you finish one lot of fibre remember to leave a fluffy end to join the next lot onto rather than spinning it right to the end. This is easier than joining when it breaks because there will be no fluffy end when it breaks.

If any join keeps pulling apart either make a loop in the yarn or tie the yarn around the fibre as described before. If one kind of fibre is hard to join, another kind will often be easier. Wool is generally easy to join on but some wool is easier than others.

how not to get a sore shoulder

The spindle does not need to be held vertically up in the air, which can be hard on the shoulders and arms. Instead try drafting on the diagonal. Eventually you can learn to draft horizontally across in front of yourself but for now drafting on the diagonal is a good habit to cultivate.

Keep on practising the techniques described above until you feel confident. Then it is time to progress to the next stage – *throwing* the spindle off the thigh.

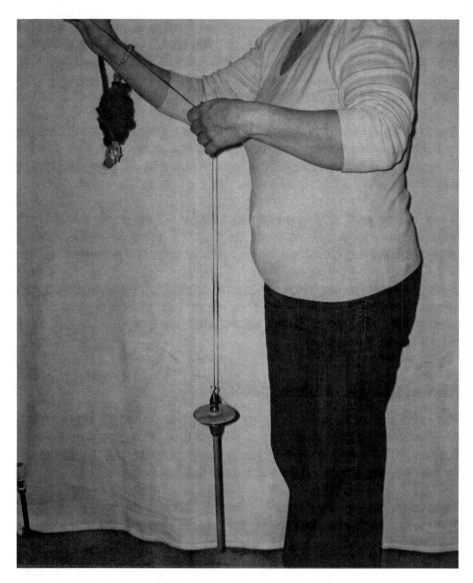

fig 38: drafting on the diagonal as opposed to vertically

how to throw the spindle off the thigh

Throwing the spindle off the thigh makes it spin much faster and keep going for longer, which is one of the reasons high tops can be so productive. This is easier than it sounds so do not be daunted by it; as soon as you can spin a bit of yarn by twirling the spindle you are ready to try it.

Wrap the yarn that is already on the spindle around the hook as usual. Hold this yarn in one hand so that the spindle is suspended from it but do not let it untwist. The other hand will throw the spindle.

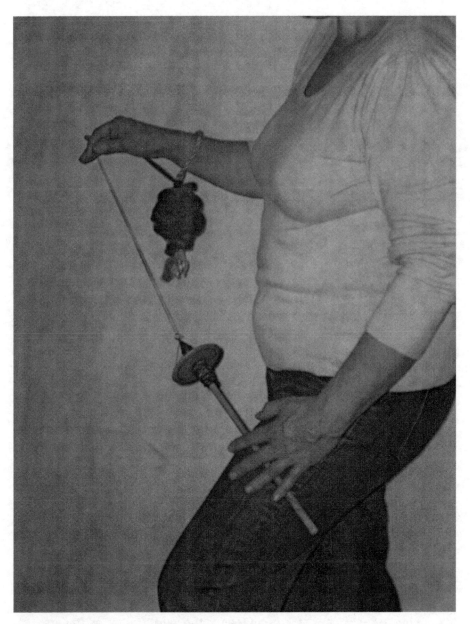

fig 39: throwing the spindle off the thigh

To make the spindle go clockwise, roll the shaft either up the right thigh or down the left thigh. It is a steady action rather than jerky, despite being called throwing the spindle.

To begin, stand up and lay the shaft across the thigh so that it is almost vertical. Hold it against the thigh with the fingers flat and lying across the shaft of the spindle, pressing it onto the thigh.

Then roll the spindle steadily from the tips of the fingers towards the palm and continue to roll with the flat of the hand. Finally, with a little flick, it becomes airborne. All this time, the yarn in the other hand is held under a slight tension and is ready to take up the slack once the spindle has been thrown.

Aim to keep the spindle as close to vertical as possible so that it can spin easily as you flick it, rather than having to right itself from a horizontal position.

Because the spindle spins much faster using this method, it is even more important that there is a decent length of yarn coming from the spindle to take up the twist. If it is too short, the spindle will spin for a short time and then unwind rapidly. In severe cases it will break.

how to kick the spindle

It helps to wear sensible footwear when doing this – some nice flat shoes with a thickish sole such as trainers are ideal. This technique makes it possible to get up serious speed and be really productive on a spindle. Because the spindle spins so fast, the twist will actually pass over your fingers with a bit of help.

Hold the yarn loosely or so that it is just suspended by a couple of fingers. Pulse the fingers if holding the yarn, or let go first with one finger and then the other if the yarn is suspended from the fingers. This helps the twist to travel over the fingers.

Holding the yarn in this way will be useful in the future if you want to do **extended draw** horizontally in front of yourself – which is a wonderful way to spin but for now just get used to feeling the yarn turn in the fingers.

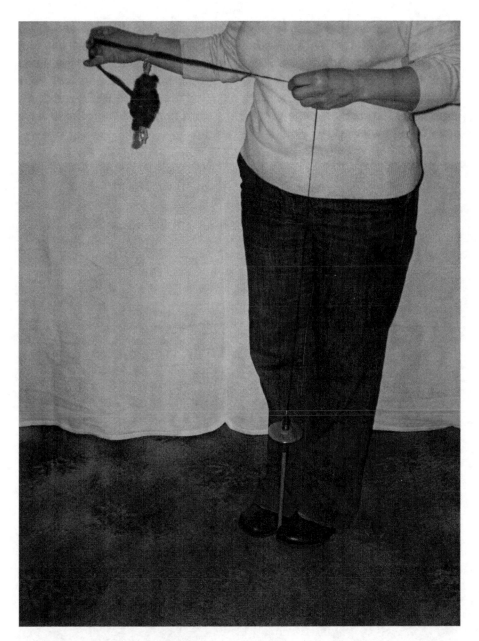

fig 40: kicking a high top spindle

To begin with, spin some yarn by throwing the spindle off the thigh. This gets a good length of yarn going and means the spindle has some momentum. See if you can feel the twist in your fingers.

Just before the spindle stops turning, lower it almost to the floor and grip it between your feet. Then either draw the right foot back or the left foot forwards with a steady action. The spindle will spin a lot faster and keep going for longer if you do this correctly. Once the hands and feet have learned to work together (i.e. without stopping the spindle whilst you draft) it gives the hands more time to draft the fibre and it is wonderful to have more time to spin before winding the yarn on.

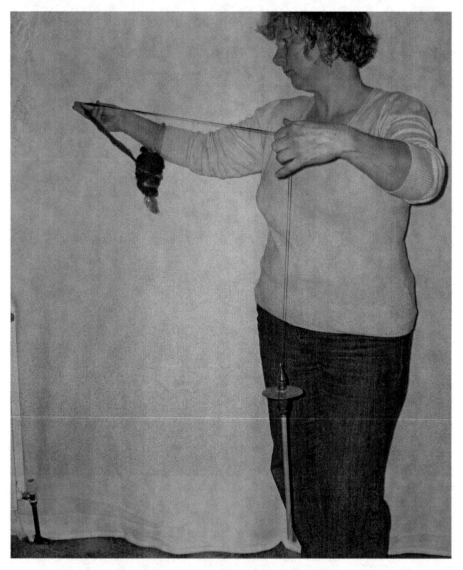

fig 41: drafting horizontally on a high top spindle

Practise drafting at an angle rather than going straight up and down. Going at an angle means you get a longer draft. You can also practise feeling the twist turn in your fingers, which it will do due to the added force of the faster spinning spindle. If you feel this happening, remember to keep one or two fingers in contact with the yarn from underneath so that the yarn is suspended from the fingers. This lets some twist through and keeps some back, meaning that you can continue drafting continuously as the twist goes into the fibre. You can 'twiddle' the fingers so that first one lets go and then the other, which helps to let the twist through.

Now that you can spin, the next step is to **ply** two strands of yarn together.

how to ply 2 or more strands together

Please also see the *how to ply on a spinning wheel* section, page 115, particularly the parts on sampling and how to fix over- and under-plyed yarn.

Once you have spun singles yarn it can be plyed by twisting it in the opposite direction so that it is a two strand yarn with more balanced twist. In certain circumstances it can be used as a singles yarn without plying.

fig 42: winding a double stranded ball for plying on a spindle

Once your spindle is full, wind the yarn you have made into a ball. To do this put the spindle on the floor then wind the yarn off by hand. Do not worry if the spindle rolls around. This is far easier than trying to get it to stay in one place.

Then spin a second spindleful of yarn. To save time, it is not necessary to wind this spindleful into a ball. Put the spindle on the floor as before but this time put the first ball of singles yarn on the floor along with it. Put the spindle on one side of you and the ball of yarn on the other so that they do not get tangled up together. Now take the end of each and wind them together into a double-stranded ball.

Put this in a cardigan or apron pocket if possible. If not, it can roll around the floor as before. Tie the two ends onto the shaft of the spindle and you are ready to ply.

When plying, spin the spindle *anticlockwise*. In other words the opposite way to when you were spinning the singles yarn.

To make four-ply yarn wind the singles yarn into two balls of double-stranded yarn and ply the two together. To get thicker yarn, spinners usually make the original two singles yarns thicker and ply those rather than making a greater number of thinner singles which takes a lot more spinning.

In certain circumstances you may want to make three- or four-ply yarns. They are pleasing to the eye because the yarn is rounded and it is also more durable which is one of the reasons Guernsey fishermen's sweaters were traditionally made from five-ply yarn.

is it essential to ply yarn?

Many spinners always ply their yarn but singles yarn has a pleasing appearance and is especially good if you are spinning a multi-coloured roving as it keeps the colours separate; although there are some tricks you can use when plying to help keep the colours separate if you do want to ply multi-coloured yarn.

When you are learning, yarn tends to be overtwisted in some places and undertwisted in others so plying is probably a good idea. Sometimes people worry that singles yarn will make their knitting slant on the bias (or diagonal). However unless it is *really* over-spun it rarely does and then only when doing plain stocking stitch knitting. Any kind of stitch pattern such as moss stitch or lace reverses the direction of the yarn so the twist is neutralised. Crochet and weaving also do this so singles yarn is fine for them.

If the yarn is to be used as singles it is best to spin it from fibre that has a staple length of at least 7.5cm (3in), otherwise it may pull apart.

a summary: tips for spindle spinning

- practise pre-drafting fibre and then twirling the spindle with scrap yarn. Do each step until you are confident before attempting the next one.
- if you struggle to join the fibre, tie a piece of yarn onto the spindle and tie this around a small amount of fibre. Either make a loop and thread a small amount of fibre through it or tie the leader yarn around the fibre. This can be done at any stage not just when starting a new spindle or bobbin and is equally useful on a spinning wheel.
- take your time. Pre-draft the fibre then spin the spindle to insert the twist. Then stop and sit down. Wedge the spindle between your knees and draft some more, rather than doing everything at once.
- if you get in a muddle or the spindle is spinning too fast, stop by lowering it onto the floor. This will give you time to draft without the spindle spinning.
- if the yarn is getting overtwisted it is important to stop immediately or it will just get worse.
- to ply, wind two lots of singles yarn into a double-stranded ball. Put this in your pocket and then ply from it.
- remember to go clockwise when spinning and anticlockwise when plying.
- refer to the section on plying yarn on a spinning wheel for some extra tips, see page 115.

how to spin on a spinning wheel

Spinning on a wheel will be broken down into stages just as it was for the hand spindle. This makes it easier than trying to do it all at once the first time.

Spinning on a wheel shares many elements with spindle spinning; the pre-drafting and drafting of the fibre are the same. The spinner must also treadle with their feet to turn the spinning wheel although there are exceptions, such as the electric spinning wheel and the charkha where the wheel is turned by hand.

make sure you get off to a good start

- if you are considering buying or making a spinning wheel, please read the *spinning wheels* chapter, page 41, to learn about the different types of wheel and how to buy one, before doing so. As a beginner it is all too easy to buy the wrong thing and end up thinking that spinning is just too hard.
- refer to the following section on lubricating a spinning wheel and make sure yours is well oiled.
- learn how to adjust the tension on your wheel before you start. This is slightly different for each type of wheel, so if you have instructions for the wheel, read any advice given here in conjunction with those.
- refer also to the *getting ready to spin: fibre* chapter, see page 63, and make sure you use only best quality, very-well-prepared medium-length wool fibre to learn with. Beginners sometimes try and 'save' their better fibre for when they have learned, but you will never learn unless you use good quality fibre.

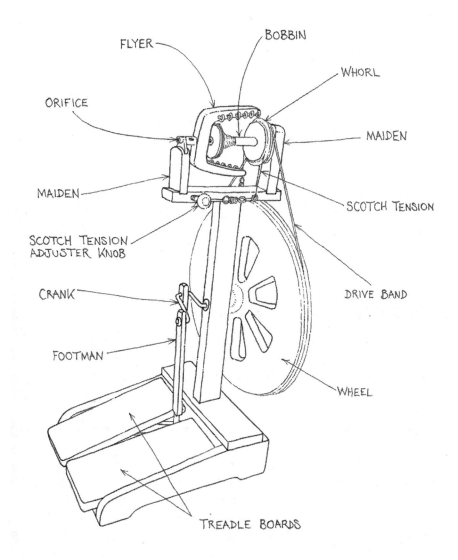

FLYER

BOBBIN

WHORL

ORIFICE

MAIDEN

MAIDEN

SCOTCH TENSION

SCOTCH TENSION
ADJUSTER KNOB

CRANK

DRIVE BAND

FOOTMAN

WHEEL

TREADLE BOARDS

fig 43: the parts of a spinning wheel

lubricate the wheel and make sure the bobbins are running free

Spinning wheels need some basic care and lubrication to keep them running well. A common reason people struggle is that their wheel has not been oiled and adjusted correctly so it is very important to do this regularly.

Refer to the diagram *the parts of a spinning wheel*, fig 43, and if the wheel came with a manual check the advice given about oiling it.

the flyer and bobbins

Some wheels have sealed-for-life ball bearings which means that in theory you only need to oil the flyer spindle where the bobbins touch it.

The *flyer assembly* is the part of the wheel that must be oiled most often. Take the flyer off the spinning wheel and oil it at either end, where it sits on the bearings (unless there are sealed-for-life-bearings). Then oil the central spindle where the ends of the bobbin rest. It is important to oil these points regularly so that any grit from fleece is removed and does not cause wear. If there is oil there already, wipe it away and re-oil. That way any remaining grit from fleece will be removed. Grit can be present even in washed fleece but not normally in tops or other commercially-prepared fibre. Make sure there is no fibre caught around the spindle or the flyer hooks.

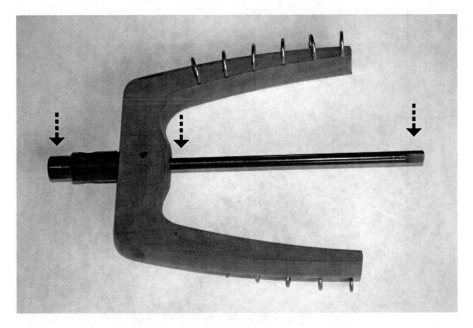

fig 44: flyer showing oil points

A wheel cannot work well unless this is done regularly so it is good to get into the habit of giving these points a little bit of oil each time you spin. A small drop on each point is enough.

the wheel hub

This does not need oiling very often. If the wheel has a hole going through the centre do not put oil in it. In this case there is actually a fixed pin that goes straight through the wheel and out the other side. The crank is fixed to the wheel by this pin and does not rotate around it. The oil will just drip out of the bottom and spoil the carpet. Instead put oil at the side of the hub where the main axle or **crank** is attached to the footman and hence the treadle board.

the treadle board ends or hinges

If there are metal pins that go from the treadle board into the legs or other fixed point, these are rubbed with candle wax when the wheel is put together. If this has been done they should not need oiling but if they squeak, try oiling them. It may work but do not over do it or the wood could swell and make it worse. Make sure the screws that hold the wheel together have not worked loose, see fig 45, as this causes flexing which can also make the treadle board ends squeak.

fig 45: treadle board viewed from underneath: arrows indicate the position of hinges which are oiled if the wheel squeaks

If oiling does not work, the treadle board needs to be taken out so that the ends can be re-waxed. To take it out one of the legs needs to be removed, which is usually straightforward. If you are a member of a group, someone with a similar wheel is likely to know how to do it. Alternatively, a spinning supplier may help as many also service and repair wheels.

Wheels such as the Majacraft Little Gem or Ashford Joy have hinges under the treadle board. If you turn the wheel over you will be able to see these and can oil them just like you would any other hinge. You will know if they need oiling because they will squeak.

In summary, the bits you need to oil regularly are the bobbin ends and the ends of the flyer where it touches the bearings. The rest is occasional and/or when there is a problem. If the wheel squeaks, it is not always obvious where the noise is coming from but the treadle board hinges are the most likely culprits.

practise treadling

Start your practice by treadling without any yarn or fibre attached. There are two types of foot control on spinning wheels – single treadle, which has one treadle board, or double treadle which has two.

double treadle wheels

On a double treadle wheel, simply place one foot on each treadle board in a comfortable position. The actual position of the feet on the treadle boards is less important than it is on a single treadle wheel. To get the wheel to go the way you want is simple – if one foot makes it go the wrong way, try the other foot. Sometimes it helps to treadle slightly with one foot and then the other, but if you practise for a few minutes the coordination you need usually becomes fairly obvious.

The majority of new wheels are now sold with double treadle as standard because it is so easy to use. Some give a choice of single or double treadle and the double treadle is usually the best choice. Single treadle Ashford wheels can be converted to double treadle by purchasing a double treadle conversion kit, so a well-priced second-hand Ashford can still be a good buy even if it is single treadle.

Louet single treadle wheels are easier to work anyway for some reason but even so, many of their wheels also now come with double treadle as standard.

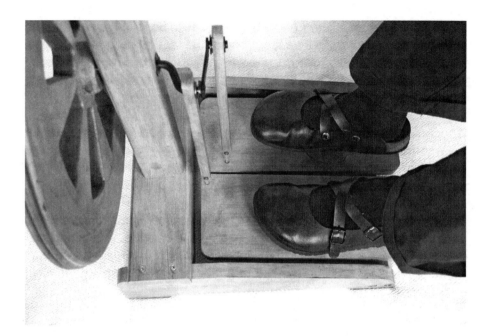

fig 46: foot position on a double treadle wheel

single treadle wheels

On a single treadle wheel there are several choices about what to do with your feet.

1. You can treadle with one foot. If you do this it is important that you keep your foot towards the back of the treadle board. Any spinning wheel worth its salt – and that means pretty much all modern ones – will have a short overhang on the back of the treadle board – that is the bit nearest to you when you are spinning. This means that you can treadle with a heel and toe action, with the heel operating the overhanging part of the board. This gives you extra control as you can then use the heel as a brake or to change direction.

2. You can treadle with one foot forward and one foot back. This makes sure that one foot is at the back of the treadle board on the overhang.

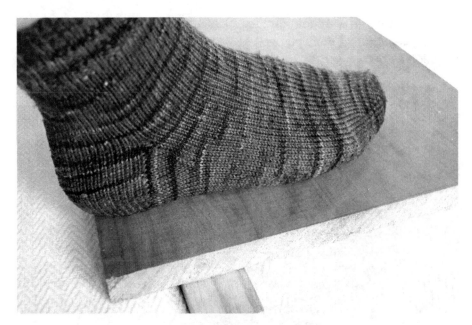

fig 47: foot position on single treadle wheel: note that the foot is to the rear of the treadle which enables the heel to be used as a brake

fig 48: treadling with one foot forward and one back

3. You can treadle with both feet together. Keep them both at the back of the treadle board so that you can use your heels as a brake and to change direction as before.

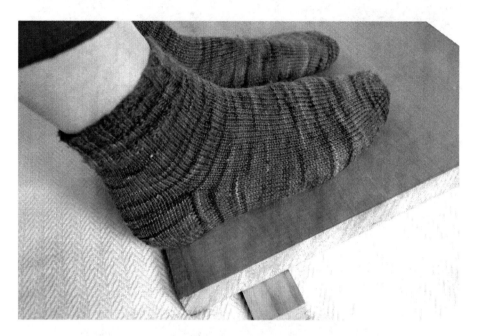

fig 49: treadling with both feet together

It only takes about ten minutes to learn good treadling control and it is well worth spending the time.

If you can already spin, treadling practice is useful when using a new wheel for the first time as wheels can be very different even if they are the same model.

Now watch what is happening when you treadle and read this in conjunction with *the parts of a spinning wheel* diagram, fig 43 page 94, if necessary. The **footman** usually comes out of the treadle board and attaches to the **crank** at the top. On an Ashford wheel the crank is a strong, bent piece of metal at the front or rear of the wheel. It and the footman join the treadle board to the wheel itself so that they all turn as one when you treadle.

On Louet wheels the footman is connected directly to the wheel by a round plastic connector and other wheels have different systems. Whichever way yours is connected, the principle is the same so have a good look whilst you treadle. It is important to know where the crank is on your particular wheel because it is used as an indicator for which way the wheel is going to turn when you start to treadle.

learn to stop and start the wheel with your feet

Good treadling control means you can stop and start treadling without using your hands, which is useful when they are busy with the fibre.

It is not easy when you begin to spin to do everything at once and anything that helps is worth using. Begin treadling with the crank at the 2 o'clock position as you look at it and the wheel will turn clockwise. Begin treadling with it at 10 o'clock it will go anticlockwise.

Start by treadling fast in a clockwise direction. As you get the hang of it, slow down until you are going as slowly as possible. Keep going slowly in a clockwise direction until you feel confident then practise using the heel as a brake. Aim to stop the wheel with the crank at the 2 o'clock position. If it goes too far, press down with the heel to bring it back up to the 2 o'clock position.

Then practise starting the wheel again without using your hands. If the wheel stopped with the crank in the 2 o'clock position it should naturally go clockwise.

Repeat the exercise going anticlockwise and stop and start the wheel with the crank in the 10 o'clock position. Ten or fifteen minutes treadling should be ample time to get the hang of it.

practise with a cone of fine yarn (pretend spinning)

The next stage is to practise feeding yarn into the wheel without actually spinning, so that the hands and feet are working together. This means you know what it feels like without having to deal with fibre as well.

Fine yarn can cope with more twist than thicker yarn. This is a fascinating fact about spinning but also a very important one and bears repeating. It means that if there are thin and thick bits in the spinning, the twist will keep going to the thin parts and the thick parts will get very little twist no matter what you do.

Find a cone or ball of reasonably fine yarn with which to practise, as it will be more tolerant of your efforts to learn. If you do not have anything very fine, just use the finest you have.

Thread the end of the yarn through the orifice and tie it around the bobbin core. Make sure it goes around the flyer hooks. These hooks lay the yarn onto the bobbin and changing hook regularly ensures that the bobbin fills up evenly. That way the yarn cannot become tangled. It also means that if you lose the end of the yarn it is easier to find.

fig 50: flyer viewed from above, showing threading of yarn onto bobbin

adjust the tension

Now that there is some yarn joined onto the spinning wheel you will be able to adjust the tension. Do this with yarn threaded through the orifice and attached to the bobbin.

There are three basic kinds of wheels: double drive, Scotch tension and bobbin lead. The tension works differently for each kind. I have all three kinds of wheel and they work equally well. A double drive or Scotch tension wheel is a better choice if you will ultimately want to spin very fine lace-weight yarns. A bobbin lead is best if you want to ultimately spin thick or fancy yarns. Otherwise any of them will do for pretty much anything you may want to spin and they are all suitable to learn on.

I am assuming here that the flyer and bobbin have already been oiled and checked for rough spots that could catch on the yarn. If it is a second-hand wheel, it should be cleaned as per the instructions given on page 57 before you attempt to adjust the tension.

If this has not been done, go back and do it now. Otherwise it will not be possible to tell whether the tension is right because dirt, lack of lubrication and rough spots might all be affecting it.

To check the tension, treadle whilst holding the yarn. The wheel should pull the yarn in fairly smartly but only when you move your hand towards the orifice. It should not feel as if you need to hang onto it. You should also be able to pull the yarn back out again with little effort and without the risk of it breaking.

If the tension is adjusted but the wheel is hard to treadle (it should feel effortless) slacken off and start again. Check for fibre caught around the flyer and bobbin hooks, oil the flyer assembly and then adjust as before.

There is one other thing to take note of here. As the bobbin fills up you need a bit more tension in order for the yarn to pull in so adjust it slightly as you go along.

double drive wheels

On double drive wheels, the drive band is a long double loop. Both loops of the band go around the wheel itself. At the other end, one part goes around the whorl at the end of the flyer and the other part goes around the end of the bobbin.

The tension is adjusted using a single large knob. Adjust it as follows: slacken off the tension until the drive band slips when you treadle.

fig 51: a double drive set up showing flyer

Then tighten it a half turn at a time until it no longer slips and the yarn is taken onto the bobbin when you move your hand forwards but can also be pulled back out easily. When you are actually spinning (or in this case feeding yarn in) it should not feel as if you have to hang onto the yarn.

Scotch tension wheels

Please refer to the diagram *parts of the spinning wheel*, fig 43 page 94, to see the location of the Scotch Tension adjustment knob.

On Scotch tension wheels, the drive band consists of a *single* loop which goes around the end of the flyer. The tension is controlled by two knobs. One controls the drive band itself and the other one – the Scotch tension - controls how the yarn is pulled through the orifice and hence onto the bobbin once it is spun.

fig 52: a Scotch tension set up

The Scotch tension adjuster normally consists of a thin bit of twine or string and one or more springs. Sometimes the springs are replaced by elastic bands and this works fine too.

The twine goes around the end of the bobbin independently of the drive band. It is usually secured by a spring at one end and a knob at the other. Any surplus twine will be wound around the knob. To adjust the amount of pull you get on the yarn, loosen or tighten this knob about a quarter of a turn at a time. Watch the spring. You want to just take the slack out of it and no more, so when it begins to move, the tension is probably about right. As you adjust the Scotch tension it may also be necessary to adjust the drive band which may slip if the Scotch tension is tighter.

The diagram *the parts of a spinning wheel*, fig 43 page 94, shows an example of Scotch tension on an Ashford wheel.

bobbin lead wheels

The third kind of wheel has just one loop of drive band that goes directly around the end of the bobbin and does not go around the flyer at all. This is called a **bobbin lead wheel.** The bobbin and flyer rotate independently of each other. When the yarn is being twisted, they both spin at the same speed. When the yarn is being fed onto the bobbin, they rotate at different speeds and the yarn is wound onto the bobbin as a result. Louet wheels work on this principle. If they are set up well they work well, although you need to use a few tricks when spinning fine yarns because bobbin lead wheels tend to exert extra pull on the yarn.

Do not let that put you off them though – they are good wheels. And you should still not feel as if you have to hang onto the yarn whilst spinning if the wheel is adjusted properly. If the wheel does still have too much pull once it is adjusted, pad the bobbins as outlined in the section on spinning lace yarn in the *spinning fine yarns* chapter, see page 191.

Bobbin lead wheels have a cradle at the front (orifice) end of the flyer assembly or **front maiden** as it is called. The flyer sits in that cradle. There is a strap that lays over the flyer orifice and this strap attaches to the front maiden with an adjustable screw. In theory the strap and screw are used to alter the tension.

Because bobbin lead drive wheels naturally exert more pull on the yarn it is sufficient to lay the strap over the flyer without fastening it down at all. If there is still too much pull, oil the cradle rather than using Vaseline as is sometimes suggested, and leave the strap off altogether.

fig 53: a bobbin lead wheel; the drive band goes around the end of the bobbin and the tension adjustment is the strap that goes over the front of the flyer

practise feeding the yarn in

Hold the yarn in whatever way is comfortable for you. Most right-handed people will want to put the cone of yarn on their left hand side and lead with the right hand. Lefthanders tend to do the opposite.

Do not let the yarn slide through your fingers, as this is not what needs to happen when you are spinning and you are aiming to mimic the actual spinning process.

Pull some yarn off the cone with one hand. Now grip it with the front hand and feed it into the orifice of the spinning wheel by moving your hand towards the orifice. Try to be conscious of your feet and to treadle slowly.

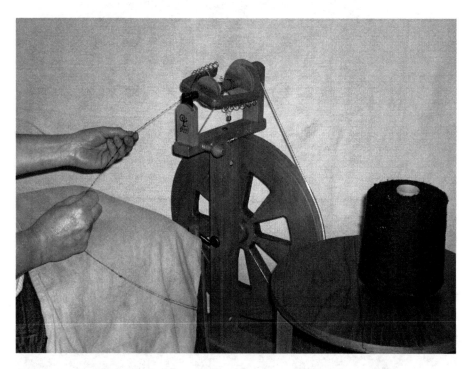

fig 54: to practise feeding yarn into a spinning wheel use a cone of fine yarn

After five or ten minutes you should have a feel for how the wheel works. Break off the yarn and get ready to start spinning for real.

pre-draft the fibre

Please refer back to *how to pre-draft the fibre for manageable spinning*, page 66. This is a similar process whether you are spinning on a wheel or a spindle.

Make sure you have practised pre-drafting until you understand what is happening and can do it fairly easily. Pre-drafting serves an additional function for wheel spinners. It means your hands do not have to work so quickly in order to keep up with your feet.

fig 55: pre-drafting fibre for spinning uses the same method whether you are spinning on a wheel or a spindle

All of the drafting can be done in advance and as a beginner that is a very good idea. Then all you need to do whilst actually spinning, is to feed the fibre into the wheel at the right speed to get the amount of twist you want.

make a 'leader'

You do not need to remove any fine yarn you have been practising with from the bobbin unless the bobbin is more than half full.

Take a piece of woollen yarn about 90cm (3ft) long. Tie this firmly around the core of the bobbin. It helps to tie it over the yarn that is already on the bobbin as this prevents it from slipping. Tuck the end of the previous yarn under it so that it does not come undone. Once you have spun your first yarn, use a piece of handspun singles – i.e. not plyed – yarn as a leader, which is the ideal, but for now a piece of commercially-spun yarn will do.

fig 56: *leader tied on to the bobbin and threaded through the orifice ready for spinning*

how to join the fibre onto the 'leader'

Please refer to fig 33, page 78, and see the instructions in the section *how to join the fibre in the spindle* section. Now that you have a nice thin, pre-drafted roving to work from it is time to join it onto the leader yarn.

Attach the fibre as follows: tie a loop in the leader using an overhand knot. If you don't know how to do one of those, just do any knot, but an overhand knot is non-slip which is useful.

Thread the pre-drafted fibre through the loop, making sure it is fairly thin, and double it back on itself. Pull back the doubled fibre so that it is the desired thickness before the twist goes into it.

Hold the doubled-back section of the fibre and treadle until there is enough twist to hold it together.

take your time: treadle, stop and draft

You do not have to do it all at once. Now the fibre is joined on, treadle a bit more and build up some twist. Pinch the yarn between thumb and forefinger though, so that the twist builds up in the spun yarn and the leader but cannot actually go into the unspun fibre. If the twist travels into the rest of the fibre before you are ready, it will no longer be possible to draft it.

Twist is what locks fibre together and changes it into yarn. So once the twist is there it is hard to make the yarn any thinner. Remember also that the twist goes to the thin places, so if the join is too thick or not long enough, the twist will not go into it and make it secure.

Once the twist has built up and the yarn looks a bit overtwisted, stop treadling. The time to stop is when you feel the yarn begin to turn in your fingers. Now gradually let the twist through into your pre-drafted fibre. Do not let it go all the way along the fibre and move your 'fibre hand' back a few inches at a time to control the twist.

If the fibre seems too thick, now is the time to draft the remaining untwisted section of the roving some more – i.e. while you are not treadling. Then treadle again and repeat...

Using a spinning wheel successfully is all about timing and does take practise. The trick to learning it quickly is to take your time and do it in stages. '*Treadle, stop, draft and then let the twist through*'. Say it as a mantra whilst spinning until you get the rhythm of it. After a while, the actions will join themselves together without any effort.

if you get stuck, stop

If the yarn stops feeding onto the bobbin, stop immediately. Otherwise it will quickly become overtwisted and become like a corkscrew. Then it will struggle to go over the flyer hooks and the situation will get worse and worse.

If this happens the best thing to do is totally remove the yarn from all of the flyer hooks. Just lift it off and put it back on again, without breaking off the yarn. This makes sure there are no invisible fibres caught on the hooks, because that is all it takes to stop the yarn from winding on.

Then wind the yarn on by hand for a little way. Try treadling briefly and see if the next bit you spin will wind on okay. If not, stop again and adjust the tension by a small amount – say a quarter of a turn. If the wheel has Scotch tension, adjust this first and then adjust the drive band as well but only if it begins to slip.

Repeat this procedure twice only. If it does not work, do not do it over and over again or the yarn will get more and more overtwisted and the tension on the wheel will get too tight.

If it doesn't work, slacken the tension off and oil the flyer and bobbin ends and then re-adjust the tension. You cannot ignore this and it has to be done systematically. Otherwise you could spend all day just trying to get the yarn to feed in and not getting any spinning done at all.

Often it is simply that beginner yarn is a little thick for the orifice, or a bit overtwisted which causes it to get stuck on the hooks. The solution is to have patience and wind the yarn on by hand whenever necessary. Eventually, as your spinning improves, it will cease to be such a problem.

some tips for wheel spinning

- lubricate the flyer and adjust the tension every time you start to spin
- use medium-length well-prepared wool fibre for learning
- pre-draft the fibre
- do not attempt to do everything at once to start with:
  'treadle, stop, draft and then let the twist through'

troubleshooting for wheel spinning

it won't wind onto the bobbin

- remove the yarn totally from the flyer hooks in case a single fibre has got caught
- check the tension; adjust as per the instructions on page 102
- check that it doesn't need oil on the flyer and bobbin ends

it is getting too much twist

- this may also be due to the yarn not winding onto the bobbin so see the tips above
- if the yarn gets overtwisted, slow your feet down. Stop treadling and let your hands catch up. Remember that your hands and feet do not need to work at the same time
- stop and wind the overtwisted yarn onto the bobbin by hand. This is very important. Otherwise the more you keep treadling, the worse it will get

it is too thick

- pre-draft until the roving is thinner and do not let the twist work its way back into the unspun section of the roving

the yarn breaks with an audible snap

- this is due to too much twist. Have a look at the tips above to do with twist
- make sure you leave at least 45cm (18in) of yarn protruding from the orifice when you wind on

the yarn drifts apart

- you are actually making progress and beginning to get the hang of it when this starts to happen
- your hands have speeded up so that your feet now need to treadle faster. The yarn also tends to get thinner as you improve and thinner yarn needs more twist to hold it together.

it feels heavy when I treadle the spinning wheel

- the tension is too tight
- oil the flyer and bobbin ends

how to ply on a spinning wheel

Plying basically means treadling so that the wheel turns in the opposite direction and twists two spun singles together to make a plyed yarn. This gives the yarn strength and balances some of the twist. This does not always matter and yarn can be used as singles.

Please also see the section *how to ply 2 or more strands together,* on page 89, in the *how to spin on a high top spindle* chapter. In particular, the discussion of when to ply yarn and when not to is equally useful to wheel spinners.

make or buy a 'lazy kate' to hold the bobbins

Some wheels have a lazy kate actually on the spinning wheel and if so it will probably look like metal rods sticking upwards. Others have a free-standing one that usually comes with the wheel. If you have bought a second-hand wheel and do not have a lazy kate, either buy or make one.

fig 57: top; improvised lazy kate made from cones of yarn and knitting needles. Bottom; Ashford upright lazy kate

One way is to push two knitting needles through a shoe box to hold the bobbins. An even easier way is to stand cones of yarn on the floor, one either side of you. Put a knitting needle through the top of the cone into the hollow centre and put the bobbin onto the knitting needle. This works best with fairly large cones as they are less likely to fall over.

fig 58: lazy kate made from a shoe box and knitting needles

put a new bobbin on the spinning wheel

Put a third, empty bobbin onto the spinning wheel and put the two full bobbins onto the lazy kate. Now thread the two ends of the yarn from the full bobbins through the spinning wheel orifice in the opposite direction to usual – i.e. from the orifice going towards the bobbin on the wheel.

Tie these ends directly onto the bobbin. If you use this method a leader is not necessary for plying.

Do not attempt to tie the ends onto any singles yarn that is already on the bobbin. Because you are going to work in the opposite direction, the singles yarn will unravel as you feed the plyed yarn onto the bobbin if you do, resulting in a tangled mess. If there is any singles yarn on the bobbin, tie the new yarn over it so that the end is trapped and this will prevent it from unravelling.

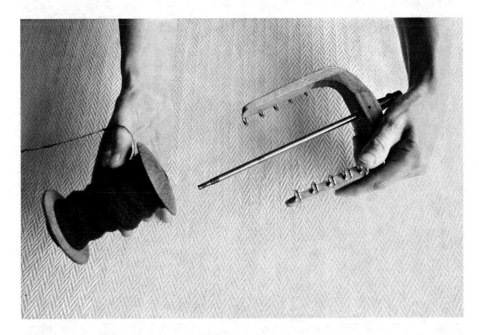

fig 59: putting a bobbin on the spinning wheel, or removing the full one, is easy

Plying is generally easier to learn than spinning, but you can get into a bit of a muddle to start with, so take your time and be prepared to stop. The first singles yarn you produce is likely to be quite thick and twisted so it may be necessary to wind some of it onto the bobbin by hand.

When plying the wheel needs to turn in the opposite direction, so if you went clockwise when spinning the singles yarn, go anticlockwise when plying.

The yarn should not slip through your fingers. Control the twist, build up twist and run that twist back with your fingers. This creates a more even yarn and prevents the spinning wheel from running away with you. Do not let go of the yarn, or the twist will go all the way back to the bobbins and tangle them together.

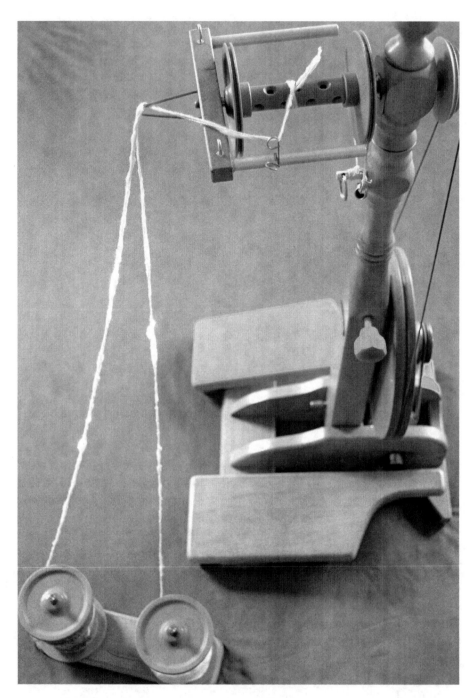

fig 60: *singles yarns in position on lazy kate; the ends of the yarns are threaded through the orifice from front to back and tied around the bobbin core ready for plying*

under-plyed is more likely than over-plyed

Because plying is easier than spinning, it is tempting to ply too quickly and not give the twist time to run into the yarn. That is why under-plying is common on both spinning wheels and spindles.

If the plyed yarn is very kinky and seems too twisted it is more likely that you have under-plyed than over-plyed. The amount of ply it takes to balance yarn depends upon the amount of twist that was put into the yarn as it was spun in the first place.

The exception is a yarn that has three or more plies because then there are three, or more, singles yarns taking up the same space as two in the yarn so it needs less twist.

take a sample

This is not essential. If it seems daunting, ply the yarn without sampling to start with. You can always come back to this section and try making a sample later.

The easiest way to make sure yarn is plyed properly is to take a freshly spun sample whilst you are spinning the singles. This only works with freshly spun yarn. The twist does not double back properly once the yarn has rested so you cannot tell if a yarn is balanced by doing this test later.

Pull off a length of the singles yarn and allow it to double back on itself. It will naturally ply until it is balanced. Hang this on the wheel or keep it with your hand spindle. When plying, simply insert twist until it looks about the same.

Count the number of treadles it takes to get the yarn to look the same. Then continue to count the same number of treadles each time you ply a length of yarn. For example, treadle seven times each time a length of yarn is fed onto the bobbin. Stop and compare it with the sample every so often as it may be necessary to add an extra treadle or two now and then.

how to fix over- or under-plyed yarn

Assume the yarn is under-plyed and try the following first. Put the bobbin of plyed yarn back on the lazy kate and run it back through the spinning wheel again going in the same direction as when it was plyed for the first time. Test a bit as you go and if it is better you are on the right track. If it seems worse, try going in the opposite direction as it may be over-plyed.

Then run the whole bobbin of yarn through the wheel again either adding more twist or taking some out. You can do this with under- or overtwisted singles yarn too.

tips for plying on a spinning wheel

- remember to go in the opposite direction to the way you went when spinning the singles yarn
- when plying with two bobbins on a lazy kate that holds three or more bobbins leave a gap between them – i.e. do not use the centre slot
- if using a free-standing upright lazy kate (i.e. the bobbins stand on end), prop something under the side nearest to you so that it is slightly tilted. A pen or pencil works quite well. This helps the yarn to flow off the bobbins without catching on the bobbin ends.
- take your time until you get the hang of it
- do not let the twist travel beyond your fingers or the strands will tangle on the lazy kate
- help any lumpy or very thick yarn by winding it on by hand; it is twice as thick when it is plyed
- if plying more than two strands, use two lazy kates and put one on either side of the wheel
- refer back to the section on *how to ply on a hand spindle* for some extra tips, see page 89

spin for 10 minutes a day and it will get done

When I first started spinning I had to get up in the middle of the night to spin because it was so exciting. At the end of a week, I had spun a rather large, White Faced Woodland tup (ram) fleece. The person who had loaned me a spinning wheel and sold me the fleece was amazed and told me many people take a year to spin a fleece. (There is no need for it to take that long, they probably only spin at monthly meetings!) Because no one had told me that, I was undaunted.

What I learned is this: the number of years you have been spinning (a question spinners often seem to ask) is irrelevant. It is the number of hours you actually put in that counts. I spin almost every day but often only for 10 minutes. It is amazing how much you get done in 10 minutes a day and the regular practice means you remember more. Once a week will still get you there but the more often you touch that wheel the quicker the spinning will improve.

When the kids were small I used to get stressed and flustered trying to get all three of them organised and ready to go out. One day I just gave up, sat down and started to spin. Calm descended immediately, as they rushed past in all directions. They finally noticed me spinning and asked what I was doing. On being told that I was spinning until they were ready to go out they all hurried up and were ready in no time. From then on, I would get myself ready then start to spin. One of them would call out 'she's spinning' and they would all hurry up and get ready to go!

So even someone with three (lively) children can find 10 minutes a day to spin...

And by the time you have spun the equivalent of a whole fleece, the spinning will be really quite good. I say the equivalent of a whole fleece because it is of course better to spin smaller amounts of a number of different things. But I did not know that when I started.

more advanced techniques

how to get different thicknesses of yarn

If you have just learned to spin and want to have some 'lighter' fun before learning more technique, just skip this bit and move on to the section on different fibres.

Once people have been spinning for a while they get into a rut and are often only able to spin one thickness of yarn, so come back to this section before you get too set in your ways. It is actually quite easy to spin different thicknesses once you know how.

the drafting triangle

The drafting triangle is the point at which the twist begins to 'bite' and the fibre becomes yarn.

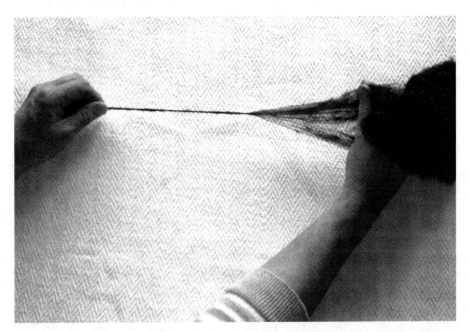

fig 61: the drafting triangle

The larger the drafting triangle, the thicker the yarn will be. This is controlled by feeding more fibre through for a thicker yarn and less for a thinner one. For a thicker yarn therefore, there needs to be a lot more fibre in front of the 'fibre hand' – the one holding the fibre – and for a thinner one, less. Remember that at all times you are drafting fibre from in front of that hand, not through it.

It helps to fan out the fibres with the fibre hand as you draft. Do this with a sideways motion of thumb and forefinger. It makes the fibres easier to draft and you can see what is happening better. This also helps to produce a smoother and less dense yarn.

the thickness and length of the fibre

The kind of fibre used will to some extent determine the range of thicknesses that can be achieved. Most fibres will give a range of thicknesses but only within certain limits. To make very fine yarn use a very fine fibre and to make a very thick one use thicker and longer fibre.

Longer fibres are useful with thick yarns because they have very little twist to hold them together. Short fibres may not have enough twist along their length for the yarn to stay in one piece.

Different types of fibre and yarn work best for different things. A Longwool yarn such as Wensleydale would be good for walking socks if it was spun fairly finely with a lot of twist. It would be hard wearing but not itchy because Longwools tend to make smooth yarns without many ends sticking out. Longwools have smoother, shiny fibres and this means the socks will not feel coarse to the wearer. The same fibre could be lightly spun for a scarf and it would feel softer.

Here is another example of how wool type can affect the end result: yarn for a baby jacket could be softly spun from something like Merino superwash tops. (The superwash means it can go in the washing machine.) Merino is soft and crimpy. It makes a stretchy yarn that is soft to the touch so long as it does not have too tight a twist in it.

The crimp and softness means it also felts well and this makes it the fibre of choice for many felt makers. Merino that is not superwash can therefore be a problem in knitwear as it tends to matt and pill.

fig 62: locks of Corriedale and Wensleydale fleece, illustrating the great range of wool fibres available

It needs the bobbles taking off regularly and does not respond well to frequent washing. One solution is to spin the yarn with a tighter twist, which reduces the problem. Another is to use superwash Merino which does not felt and tends to pill less.

Another alternative is to blend the Merino with something else such as silk. This makes a more durable yarn because although silk is a luxury fibre it is actually very hard wearing. It massively reduces the tendency to pill and felt too. You can buy pre-blended Merino and silk tops in many different colours so this is an easy solution.

And of course a different fibre could be used to start with. Bluefaced Leicester tops are a good choice because they are also nice and soft but do not pill nearly as much as Merino. This is because Bluefaced Leicester is actually in the **Longwool and lustre** group of fibres and the wool is smoother and a bit shiny.

Do not try to spin Bluefaced Leicester into a smooth yarn straight from a fleece though – buy it as tops. It is a mass of small curls and takes a very long time to comb out. You will end up frustrated, bored and with sore fingers! A Bluefaced Leicester fleece can, however, be spun directly from the curls without carding and made into a wonderful, textured curly yarn.

Do not fight the nature of the fibre and if you do struggle to get the yarn you want, try spinning something else.

the amount of twist

The amount of twist also affects thickness. Here is a simple exercise to help you learn about it.

Spin a length of yarn but do not feed it into the orifice. Double a small piece back on itself and let it ply itself together. Break this sample off and lay it on your leg.

Now do the same again. This time treadle six to eight more times so that there is more twist than before. Let the sample ply back on itself and compare the two. The second one should be thinner and have a tighter twist in the plyed yarn.

Make a third sample in the same way but this time with less twist than the first one. To do this treadle fewer times.

There should now be 3 samples that look quite different. The one with the tightest twist will be the thinnest one. The thinnest one will also feel harder and maybe a bit stiffer to the touch and the one with the least twist will be the softest.

Hardness or softness which is caused by the amount of twist rather than the nature of the fibre is called the *handle* of the yarn.

spinning from the fold or over the finger.

This is enjoyable and leads to a fluid and fast spinning style. It is best done on a spinning wheel, as the frequent joins become tedious on a hand spindle. Spinning from a pencil roving is an effective and fluid way of using a high top spindle in any case.

Some people find it easier to start with a pencil roving as previously described, see page 68, whilst others find it easier to spin from the fold, which just goes to show we are all different. So if you have struggled with the pencil roving method, try this.

Spinning from the fold or over the finger makes some combed tops or rovings easier to spin because once they are folded in half, the fibres are no longer all going in the same direction. So if a particular fibre is hard to spin as a pencil roving, try it this way. It will work with any fibre that is 6.5cm (3in) or longer.

It is an especially useful method when spinning longer fibre as folding it halves the length and makes it easier to spin.

New fibre needs to be joined on much more often using this method. However, joining new fibre confidently is a core skill in spinning. Once learned, it will stop you worrying about the yarn or fibre pulling apart and you will not to hold on to it so tightly. So learning this method will improve your spinning no end and after a couple of hours you will no longer even think about those joins.

pull off one staple length of fibre

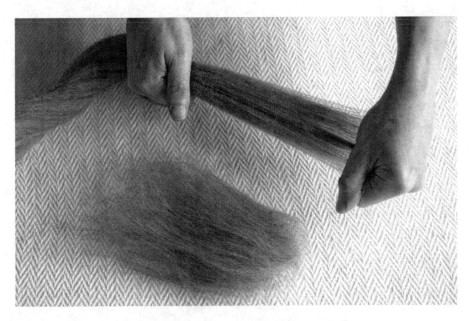

fig 63: pulling off one staple length of fibre from a combed top

Start by pulling off one staple length of fibre, just like you did when checking the length of the fibres earlier, see page 66. If a big chunk comes away at once, or if there may be more than one length, hold it at the very ends – one end in each hand – and pull again. Repeat this until it is obvious that there is only one staple length. It should be an average of 5-8cm (2-4in) long and the fibres should have all separated from one another. When this is done correctly the fibres will fan out and look a bit 'floaty'.

It is important that you have only one staple length or this technique will not work properly so do not be tempted to try it with a larger lump of fibre.

holding the fibre

There are two similar ways to hold the fibre when using this technique – *from the fold* or **over the finger**. Both do essentially the same job. The fibre needs to be held very loosely whichever method you choose or it will not work properly. Some people find spinning from the fold easier and some find spinning from over the finger easier. Spinning from the fold can be done with shorter fibre than over the finger.

from the fold

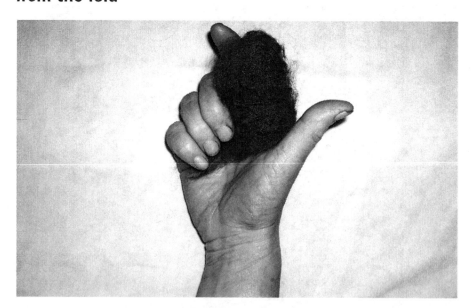

fig 64: *when spinning from the fold the fibre is held loosely by the three fingers indicated and the thumb and forefinger occasionally act as a 'brake'*

Start by folding the fibre in half. Open the hand that will hold the fibre and turn it palm up with the fingers close together but not tense. Lay the folded fibre across the fingers of your open hand with the fold next to the index finger and protruding just beyond it and the rest of the fibre going across the fingers towards the little finger, see fig 64.

Then hold it gently by curling the middle, ring and little finger of your hand around it. If it is held too tightly, the fibres do not come out in the correct order and get tangled up. Imagine you are holding a live bird and do not want to crush it. If your hand or the fibre gets hot, it is being held too tightly. If the fibre starts coming from the inside rather than the outside of the folded fibre, or from the end rather than the fold, it is also being held too tightly. It takes a bit of practice and at the beginning all of these things are likely to happen.

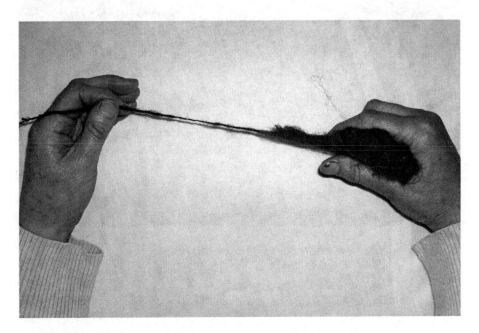

fig 65: hand position for spinning from the fold

The thumb and index finger have another job to do. They do not hold onto the fibre but act as a brake if too much fibre comes away at once.

In actual fact, the thumb is a bit of a menace as it tends to want to hang on to the fibre. It is said that if you put a clothes peg on your thumb it helps you to spin better by keeping it out of the way.

over the finger

When spinning over the finger, the thumb and the forefinger act as a brake but do not hold onto the fibre, just like when spinning from the fold. They have an additional task though and that is to work the fibre forwards so that it is always right at the tip of the finger. As when spinning from the fold, the fibre needs to be held very loosely.

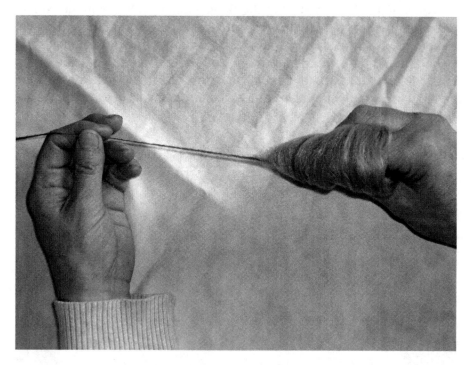

fig 66: hand position when spinning over the finger

more about fibre

Once you know the basics there is every reason to try out some different fibres. As well as learning more quickly, it will be a whole lot more fun – which is, after all, the point. I have started with those that are easier to spin, although we are all different and what one person finds easy another may find hard. Do not be put off therefore if a particular fibre does not work for you – just try something else.

dealing with fleece

The smell and feel of fleece is the reason quite a number of people learn to spin. It is a beautiful, relaxing smell and most spinners want to spin at least some fibre that they have prepared from scratch. There is no need to do so if you do not like raw fleece, as there is plenty of pre-prepared fibre available. If you do like it, there's a unique experience waiting for you – provided you learn how to work with the fleece. Otherwise it could end up as a matted, solid mass that is very hard to use.

If you do not have anyone to show you what to do, I recommend you try spinning with **medium pre-prepared wool** (i.e. combed top or pre-carded fibre) before attempting to wash and card a fleece. Please refer to the *pre-prepared fibres* section of the *getting ready to spin: fibre* chapter, page 64, for more detail if you have not done so already. That way you can learn to spin without having to deal with a fleece and learning to card at the same time.

If you do have someone to show you that is a different matter, but it has to be the right fleece, prepared well for it to be suitable for a beginner.

When you decide to try some raw fleece, start with medium-quality (i.e. the thickness of the fibres should be medium rather than fine or coarse) fleece in good condition and 7.5-10cm (3-4in) long fibres. Fleeces have an uncanny knack of finding new and unwary spinners though so here is some advice on what to look for.

how to select a good fleece

Here's one reason why spinners get offered so many free fleeces. The Wool Marketing Board pays farmers very little for fleece and next to nothing for coarser fleece. Farmers may be charged a collection fee that is more than they get paid for coloured fleeces and it is not viable to send small quantities of any fleece to the Board. This leaves the farmer with a disposal problem and many fleeces end up being dumped or burned.

Resist the farmer's helpful suggestion that you could take all 47 fleeces from his hill sheep and pass them on to spinning friends. Those friends will unroll them, take one look and reject them and you will be left with them in your garage for years. Fleece from hill sheep, such as Blackface or Swaledale is used mainly for carpets. It is hardwearing and usually too coarse for knitwear. There are much nicer things to spin. Some Cheviot fleeces can be quite nice and there are always exceptions – but you would probably still not want them next to the skin. If you want to spin for woven rugs or tapestry the coarser wool is ideal.

choosing wool for sustainability

The wool market began to decline a few years ago due to the increased use of synthetic fibres. At the time of writing it is hopefully making a bit of a recovery. This is partly due to natural fibres becoming more fashionable and partly to it being a sustainable and fire-resistant product which is increasingly being used for carpets and environmentally-friendly insulation.

Merino wool is often imported and in some countries can be a threat to local wool production. If you live in a country that produces Merino then it is a good choice. If you do not, look to the local alternatives where possible. In the UK Bluefaced Leicester is a great alternative to Merino and can be used in the same way for spinning or felt making. For spinning it is better, as it is less likely to pill and has more lustre. It is not available pre-prepared in as many colours as Merino but the range of fibres for spinners is increasing all the time.

explain what you are looking for

What you can do is to explain beforehand that you just want one fleece because it takes such a long time to spin them by hand. Tell the farmer or smallholder that you are looking for a fleece that has an open texture, is relatively free of debris and is not from a mountain or hill breed. Many farmers think a good fleece is one that is nice and firm – and that's the opposite of what spinners want. We want the one that is falling apart because it is so loose.

express your appreciation

If the fleece turns out to be a good one, bake the farmer a cake by way of thanks and tell all your spinning friends to get in touch – they will be delighted and everyone ends up better off.

some tips about fleeces

- a fleece is always best bought face to face, unless it is from a trusted supplier who knows about spinning.
- if it is a freebie, describe in advance what you are looking for, be grateful and take just one fleece rather than lots. You will probably get a bit of good stuff out of it but there might not be much. Sometimes only a handful. The rest can mulch the rhubarb or fruit trees or line hanging baskets.
- when buying a fleece, get the supplier to unroll it for you rather than attempting to do it yourself. It is possible to damage the fleece formation by doing this wrong and if that happens they will not be pleased.
- fleeces are usually rolled up inside out. They can look lovely that way up but be awful when turned 'weather' side out, so always check.
- do not lay fleeces down on debris such as straw, sawdust or cut grass
- fleeces should be open in texture, not matted and not too dirty – unless it is a Wensleydale or other Longwool fleece; they are always dirty and it washes out a treat.
- look out for hayseed and other such debris as it is very difficult to remove, unless the fibre is going to be prepared by combing rather than carding. (This process is explained later on, see page 155). Combing is best done on fleece that is 10-12.5cm (2-4in) long for mini combs and 13cm (5in) or longer for full-sized combs, so any fleece with fibres shorter than 10cm which also has a lot of debris in the wool is best rejected.
- coarse fleece from mountain and hill sheep is mainly used for carpets. Some can be good enough for knitwear if only the softer parts are used or if the fleece is from a young animal. Cheviot is a good example of fleece that is often be used for both carpets and knitwear.

sorting and washing a fleece

Having got a good quality fleece, it needs to be handled correctly to stay in good order. The aim is to have the structure of the fleece largely intact once it has been washed.

A fleece consists of **staples**. These are little sections of fibre that form locks. They usually, but not always, taper to a point at the **tip** end that was on the outside when the fleece was on the sheep. The cut **butt** end is blunter and was next to the sheep's skin before shearing.

When the fleece is carded, individual staples should stay aligned in roughly the same direction. Keeping the fleece tidy when it is sorted and washed therefore makes the carding much easier.

sorting a fleece

It is a good idea to get any fleece out of the bag and sorted as soon as possible as it can have dung on it which attracts flies.

Cover any cuts whilst handling fleece and wash your hands afterwards. Be aware that fleeces can have thorns in them from hedges so handle them gently and be aware that thorns do not always make themselves obvious when you sort or wash a fleece and may still be there later. I have often found them whilst rinsing a fleece after washing.

First of all, put the fleece on a clean surface. It will be greasy and dirty so it is a good idea to put it on an old sheet or tarpaulin. Do not put it down on anything such as a lawn or straw where there are bits or it will pick them up. It is surprisingly hard to remove these bits. Wear an apron to prevent the grease from marking clothes and have a bag to hand for any waste.

unroll the fleece

Fleeces are folded sides-to-middle then rolled up with the inside out. The neck wool is twisted into a long length and wrapped around the fleece, then the end is tucked in.

To unroll the fleece, look carefully until you find the end of this twisted length of neck wool. Take out the end and unroll the fleece from there. It is well worth having a good look until you find the end – at first glance it might not seem obvious but it really helps to keep the fleece tidy if you unroll it properly.

The unrolled fleece will still be folded sides-to-middle. Open the sides out carefully as the fleece may want to stick together. Check which is the outside (pointy tips to the locks) and which is the inside (blunter ends to the locks where it was shorn from the sheep). Then you will know that you are unfolding it correctly. Take your time to avoid getting it tangled up.

skirting

The next job is to *skirt* the fleece. This is where you harden your heart and take off everything that is not up to standard. If this is not done, the spinning process becomes much harder and less enjoyable. Just pull the waste fleece off by hand.

There is usually quite a lot of waste from a fleece, but this can be composted or used in the garden. Rhubarb, fruit trees and soft fruit bushes love it because it releases nitrogen slowly as it decomposes. The organic gardener Lawrence Hills used to recommend digging in mattress shoddy or the horsehair stuffing from old chairs around fruit trees in the days when you still got such things. Reject fleece does the same job.

The sheep is shorn starting with the middle of the belly, going up one side and then up the other. This results in the belly wool being at the two outer edges of the fleece once it is off the sheep. In other words, the outer edges consist of the wool that the sheep has been sitting on and trailing through the muck for a year so get rid of it. Even if it looks okay it will have debris in it and be matted in places. So just go right around the fleece and remove a 7.5cm (3in) strip from the edge. Do this by holding the wool to be removed in one hand and the main fleece in the other. Then use your hands to separate the wool fibres gently. Where it is dirty or matted remove more if necessary.

The rear end of the sheep has the coarsest and dirtiest wool so remove this on the way round, then stand back and have a look at the rest of the fleece.

The centre of the back may be matted. It can also be **weathered** which makes it brittle. This is because the wool on the back is constantly exposed to the elements. If the sheep has been well looked after and had access to a barn with an overhead hay rack, it will have pulled hay from the rack and showered its back with seeds. These are all but impossible to get out. So remove any problem parts from the centre back and while you are at it take out any bits that have dye on them from when the sheep was marked by the shepherd.

There will still be plenty of wool left from most fleeces after sorting. Occasionally there will be one that does not have enough left to make a sweater but it can still be used for something smaller. It is common for between a third and a half of the fleece to be discarded.

grade the wool

This is not essential and need only be a rudimentary task. If the wool is sorted too much there will not be enough of any one kind left for a project. It is worth knowing a bit about the different qualities of the wool and whereabouts they are on the sheep though and invaluable if you ever want to spin very fine yarn – because only the finest of wool from a fine fleece is used for that.

The neck wool is normally the finest and spinners sometimes reserve this for a special project. It can be in very small, bitty locks though and is not always easy to work with. If it is a fiddle, discard it or use it in a felt-making project. Fine spinning requires fine fleece that is fairly long and has well-defined but loose locks.

The rump can sometimes have short, chalky *kemp* fibres in it. Anything with these in should be discarded. They will shed while you spin, shed whilst you knit and shed when you wear the garment. They also do not take dye easily so will stand out in all their coarseness if you dye the wool.

There is often only a small amount of wool that is significantly coarser than the rest of the fleece but it varies.

You have, of course, already discarded anything that is matted but just a reminder – do not try to card and spin matted fibre. It cannot be fixed by carding, is hard to spin and does not yield good results. Get rid of it.

spin in the grease?

Now that the fleece has been sorted, it is much easier to deal with. You can spin it without washing it at all. It used to be much commoner to spin in the grease than it is now, but this was when there was little choice in the way of pre-prepared fibres in the 1970s when hand spinning as a hobby first began to take off.

Spinning in the grease causes grease to build up over time in the orifice and on the hooks of the spinning wheel. Spindle spinners need to be careful that grease does not get on clothes or furniture and this defeats the whole point of spindling being something you can do anywhere without any special equipment – who wants to carry a spinning apron in their bag?

Another drawback is that not only is the grease still present but so is the *suint* or sheep sweat. This is a dark-coloured, sticky substance that holds all the grit and debris in the fleece. The grit causes wear on the hooks of a spinning wheel and over time these may develop sharp grooves as a result. When a white fleece has been spun in the grease and is then washed, it does not come up truly white because some of the dirt is trapped by the twist.

If you do enjoy spinning in the grease, make sure the fleece is properly sorted as described above. Just pulling wool out of an unexplored bin bag is never going to yield good results.

do not use raw fleece on your 'best' carders

If carding unwashed (or raw) fleece, reserve a pair of carders solely for this purpose. This is because the grease and suint will eventually set and you will never, ever get it off again.

Eventually the carders will become difficult to use because the stickiness makes the wool catch on the carder teeth. Card cloth (the rubber fabric with the carder teeth in it) cannot be scrubbed or soaked without spoiling it. If you have a pair of carders in this condition, perhaps because you have bought a second-hand pair, the card clothing can be replaced.

For the same reason, never use unwashed fleece on a drum carder as they cost a lot more than ordinary carders and it is difficult to replace their card cloth. (A drum carder is a large carder with a handle that you turn to card the fleece.)

not after Christmas

The golden rule is, do not spin in the grease after Christmas. Sheep are shorn in May to July and by January the grease is beginning to set and the suint will be getting sticky. This makes the fleece hard to work with and you will be hauling at a yellow, sticky mass of fleece which will never produce good yarn.

If you have a fleece that has been in the attic for two years, open it out in the garden not the house. Evict the mice and other flora and fauna and give it a decent burial. Now get a nice new one and start again. Sorry, but it just doesn't keep. Once the suint has set, it is hard even to wash it out with hot water and the results are mediocre at best.

use protection

When spinning in the grease, wear a spinning apron and ensure the fleece does not come into contact with clothes or furnishings. Do your best to keep the dog out of it (good luck with that one!) and cover any cuts. Be aware that there may be thorns from a hedge caught up in the wool so handle it lightly. Always wash your hands after handling raw fleece.

Having said all this, a really lovely fleece, freshly shorn can be an absolute delight to spin in the grease.

washing a fleece

Whether cold or hot washing, the fleece should be contained in buckets or bowls rather than being allowed to spread out freely in a large bath. Otherwise it is hard to keep it tidy and the staple formation will be lost, making it difficult to deal with when it is being carded and spun.

cold-soak method

Cold soaking leaves some of the grease but gets rid of the suint along with most of the grit and dirt. Much of the remaining grit will drop out as the fleece is carded and spun, so the yarn is much cleaner and will come truly white when washed. Cold-washed wool will not make carders sticky. Merino or Longwools need special treatment and cannot be cold washed because the grease in them is different.

Cold-washed fleece feels lovely to work with. Even better, once the fleece is cold washed it will store without going sticky. I sort and cold wash all fleece as soon as I get it, then it will keep, so long as it is checked regularly.

To cold wash fleece, fill a bucket with cold water and separate out enough wool to almost fill the bucket. A fleece will usually fit into two buckets unless it is very large. It is surprising how much will go in as it takes up less room when wet. If the weather is poor and you have restricted drying room, wash and dry one bucketful at a time rather than dealing with the whole fleece at once.

Leave it in the buckets to soak for about 8 hours or overnight. Then drain it if possible. I use an old dish-draining rack which sits in the bath. The fleece is tipped into it from the bucket, water and all rather than lifting it out. This avoids disturbing that precious staple formation. It is then left to drain for a while.

If you do not have a draining rack, tip it out into the bath or onto a debris-free surface outside. If you are using the bath, get a plug-hole strainer to catch any bits of wool and prevent them from going down the drain. The water will be dark and it is amazing how much dirt comes out. Once the wool has drained it can be squeezed gently but do not agitate it too much.

Fill the buckets again and carefully push the wool back in. Avoid stretching, pulling and dunking as this will felt the wool and tangle it up. Just push it in and leave the water to do the work.

Drain as before and then repeat. Two rinses should get most of the dirt out. It is not necessary to keep rinsing until the water is completely clear but it should look a lot better and will be opaque rather than dark brown.

Put the wool into an old pillow case or net bag and tie the top. A shoe lace works well for this because it is easy to undo again later. Give the wool a gentle spin in the washing machine. Do not let the machine run for its whole spin cycle though – stop it after a short while.

Take the wool outside and spread it out – I use a picnic table – or hang it indoors over a clothes airer. If it is outside, keep an eye on it, as it may blow away in windy weather.

Once the wool is totally dry, store it in a pillow case or bag. Some people avoid storing wool in plastic bags, but as long as it is properly dry and is not in sunlight it should be fine.

hot-soak method

This removes most or all of the grease. The wool will still feel different to commercially-scoured wool. The chemicals that are used commercially strip some of the cuticle from the outside of the wool fibre whereas this does not happen with home washing. The wool fibres will feel smoother than commercially-prepared fibres and will still have a nice, gentle, woolly smell.

The most important thing is not to agitate the wool in any way or shock it by sudden changes in water temperature as this will felt or matt it. Many a fine fleece has been ruined by vigorous washing and there is a greater risk of this with hot washing than with cold.

If you have not dealt with a fleece before, or have had poor results from hot washing fleeces in the past, my advice would be to cold wash your fleece. If a fleece has been stored for some time, you may need to hot wash it in order to get all the suint out of it, as this will have gone sticky in storage.

Fill a bucket or two with water as before only this time use hot water at about 30°C and use a small amount of washing detergent. Wool wash liquid works well, but anything will do.

Read the instructions on how to cold wash fleece starting on page 139 and take all of the same precautions to avoid tangling the fleece and losing the staple formation.

Immerse the dry wool in the hot water and leave to soak as before. Once the water has cooled, proceed as for the cold soak method.

fleece that needs special treatment

Merino fleece needs special treatment due to the heavy grease in it. Do not attempt to wash a whole fleece at once. Instead, pull out individual locks and wash these one at a time with very hot water and some washing up liquid or wool wash applied directly to each lock. Rinse the locks one at a time by swishing them briefly in water of the same temperature then pat them dry and lay them on a towel to dry.

Longwool fleece such as Wensleydale has a lot of grease in it but can be washed like a normal fleece using the hot-water method, rather than cold. It will look very dirty when first purchased but do not let that put you off, the dirt will wash out. Longwool will need more rinses than other fleeces. It is really the only type of fleece you would still buy if it was very dirty.

Neither Merino nor Longwool fleeces tend to spin well without washing because of the grease. Although sometimes Merino can be wonderful to spin in the grease, especially in warmer weather, so there can be no hard and fast rules about it.

types of wool

Most people think of wool when they first begin to spin and although there are many other fibres you can use, wool is still the staple diet (pun intended) for most spinners. It is a versatile, breathable fibre that dries easily. There are so many different kinds and grades of wool that there is a type that is suitable for most things.

The British Wool Marketing Board grades the wool and sheep breeds into seven different categories, which are: Mountain, Hill, Cross breed, Medium, Fine, Lustre and Coloured fleece.

These categories are for marketing and sales purposes and therefore apply to the different ways in which wool is used commercially. For example Jacob wool is listed as *coloured*. This makes perfect sense for marketing purposes but is not much help to spinners and Jacob fleece would fit into the *medium* category if it weren't for its colour.

use common sense

Spinners must therefore use common sense when assessing an individual fleece and the Wool Marketing Board categories are at best a general guide.

The factors to consider when selecting suitable wool for projects are:

- the **fineness** (or micron count) of the actual fibres. Fibre is measured in microns and the smaller the number the finer the fibre is. It can also be measured by the *yarn count*. This is based on the number of hanks of a certain size that can be spun from the fibre. The finer the fibre, the more hanks that can be spun from it, so 100s Merino is finer than 64s.

- **softness**. This is related to fineness, as finer fibres are usually also softer. Longwools are not fine but can be soft, because the actual fibres are smooth and shiny although they are thicker.
- **length of staple**. The length of staple helps to determine how the yarn should be spun and what it is suitable for. Very short fibres are not suitable for thick singles yarns because the yarn tends to come apart. Short fibres are also less suitable for projects that need hard wearing yarn and cannot be spun from the fold or over the finger. They are great for spinning long draw though. Long fibres are not suitable for long draw spinning, nor spinning on a Charkha.
- **lustre** (or shine). Lustre is important to the look of a project. Wools with lustre are hardwearing without being coarse, providing there is not too much twist in the yarn.
- Jacob is a good example of a **fleece that varies**. It can be fine or coarse, long or short but would not normally have much in the way of lustre. Sometimes the brown parts of the fleece are coarser than the white parts. The colour variations make it fun to spin and it produces knitwear quite unlike anything that can be bought.

mountain

Mountain breeds include the coarsest of wools and are often seen on the hills because they are hardier. The wool is commonly used for carpets and home insulation.

The sheep themselves are able to withstand harsher conditions than some other breeds. Many, such as Blackface, Swaledale and Hebridean are double coated. This means their fleece has two types of fibre: a longer hair fibre which can be 10cm (4in) to 17.5cm (7in) long. This is the coarser part of the fleece. There is also an under coat which is shorter and softer. If you use wool combs on a double-coated fleece the softer part will be left behind in the combs, so carding works best.

As with any wool, the quality varies: I had some surprisingly lovely gifts of Blackface fleece when I was a new spinner and spun and knitted wonderful socks – its hard-wearing qualities have been an advantage for those. (Yes, I succumbed too.) Hebridean is one of my favourite fleeces and for some reason it has an especially wonderful smell.

There are some truly awful, coarse, matted Blackface and Hebridean fleeces, but some equally awful Shetland and Merino ones too, so it pays to shop around.

hill

The hill breeds include Cheviot, White Faced Woodland and Black Welsh Mountain.

These are useful fleeces and can all be of suitable quality for knitwear if selected with care. They are not as coarse as fleeces from the mountain breeds.

Fleeces from hill sheep can often be spun without carding and will not felt or pill easily, which is a great advantage for knitwear. A quality fleece in this category is easy to spin and makes good multi-purpose yarn.

The first fleece I spun was a White Faced Woodland. Many years later, the wool was dyed in pastel shades and I knitted a cot blanket with it. The blanket had wide pastel stripes, each with a row of sheep knitted in black Shetland and a moss stitch border. Apart from the very first hank, the yarn was actually quite well spun and very usable although at the time it was spun I had discarded it thinking it was not good enough – a common beginner's trait.

The wool from that fleece was nice and soft but also washed well and, as I now know, a cot blanket was an ideal first project because it does not have to fit.

cross breeds

Crosses between two breeds of sheep are called *mules*. Mules are usually a cross between a hill sheep such as a Blackface sheep and a larger, lowland tup (or ram) such as the Bluefaced Leicester. The breeds are crossed to increase the size and number of lambs and/or the quality of the fleece.

This is good news for spinners as crossing the Blackface with a Bluefaced Leicester produces a lovely fleece. It is softer and shinier (has more lustre) than a Blackface but also less curly than a Bluefaced Leicester. There are other crosses too and many make good spinning, so do not be put off by the fact a fleece has no special name.

medium

There are lots of good multi-purpose fleeces in this category. Both crosses and medium fleeces tend to have finer fibres and feel softer than those in the Hill category.

Examples of medium fleeces are Romney, Lleyn and Texel. These are all for knitwear rather than felt making, which means that they keep their condition well when knitted up without getting bobbly and felted.

I spun and knitted a sleeveless cardigan from Romney wool in 1998 and sold it to a friend. When we met recently she was wearing it. It showed no real signs of wear, although she has worn it often.

The Guild to which I belong took part in an event called the *fleece-to-jumper challenge*, which is an annual worldwide competition to spin and knit a sweater in a day. We used a Texel fleece without carding. It spun up as if it had been carded and needed no pre-drafting or other treatment. Medium quality fleeces are often open and more likely to be usable without carding than finer types.

fine

This category includes many of the short wool and down sheep, although not all of these have fine wool and some of the fleeces, such as Dorset Horn, can have quite a crispy feel to them. Suffolk and Clun Forest are other examples of fine fleeces.

Sheep in this category are normally less hardy than the hill breeds and need lusher, lowland conditions to thrive. Shetland could potentially be in this category except that it is classified as a coloured breed instead and Merino and related breeds give the finest wool of all.

Fine wools usually have more *crimp*, or tiny waves, in them and crimp is one of the defining characteristics of both Shetland and Merino. The wool should have a minimum number of crimps to the inch in order to be a fleece true to the breed.

Merino fleece needs special treatment so please read the *fleece that need special treatment* section, page 140, before attempting to wash it.

lustre

This group is often known as Longwool and lustre because all of the Longwool breeds are in this category, including Bluefaced Leicester.

Although lustre wools have thicker fibres, they are smooth and shiny. They make hard-wearing knitwear that is also soft, so long as it is not spun with too tight a twist, when it makes excellent pot scrubbers! Examples of Longwool breeds are Wensleydale, Cotswold and Lincoln Longwool. These are the sheep that look like they have dreadlocks, sometimes down to the ground. Only the first fleece from young sheep is this long so check it is 'first clip' if buying unseen.

Make sure you read the instructions on washing Longwools before attempting to use them, see page 140, – they really do need a hot wash.

coloured

Coloured fleece is anything that is not white. As mentioned earlier, all coloured fleeces could also be classified in one of the other sections. One helpful distinction is native and rare breeds which are much more likely to be coloured sheep.

The United Kingdom has more sheep breeds than any other country according to the British Wool Marketing Board. It is great fun to try spinning wool from different breeds and many spinners have rare-breed sheep, so it is not hard to get hold of the fleeces.

My Guild spins at an agricultural show each year and we are usually in the wool tent, along with the Wool Marketing Board and the fleece competition. (Yum.)

Sometimes we are able to purchase the fleeces after the show for a very reasonable price or even get given them free – the farmers have already sent the rest of their clip away for processing by the time the show takes place and have no further use for them. Most of us have more than enough fleece at home but usually manage to take some home rather than see it go to waste.

Shetland comes in more colours than any other breed and the colours have nice names like Badger and Moorit. The breed society produces a lovely poster with pictures of all the different colours.

Some native breeds still have the natural ability to shed their fleece whereas most modern breeds have lost this ability and must be shorn or they will eventually die. Some Shetlands still shed their fleece and Soay sheep always do. Soays look a bit like small goats and used to be an important resource on the very isolated island of St Kilda. The fleece can be pulled off once it is ready to part company with the sheep, a skill that is called **rooing**.

Native breeds tend to be hardy and some are named after Scottish Islands. The Ronaldsay is one such and the sheep live on the beaches of several islands in Scotland where their diet includes seaweed. When they are fed on grass rather than seaweed it is said they need copper supplements because they are so well adapted to their island diet.

spinning fibre without carding or other preparation

Some fleeces can be spun without any preparation other than sorting and washing although most will benefit from some carding.

Fleece to be spun without carding should not be at all stuck together at the tips, which get most of the weather when the wool is on the sheep. It helps if the fleece has a **blocky** tip – i.e. it has a blunt end at the tip rather than it going to a point.

For the fleece to be suitable, the individual staples need to be loose and easy to tease apart. The fibre can be spun just as it comes, usually from the side of the staples rather than the end, or it can be teased and drawn out into a roving by hand before spinning. Texel fleece can often be spun without carding.

how to card fibre

Carding can seem tricky if you have never seen it done. Using the correct fibre – and not too much of it – is crucial to success. The photos I have included should help but it takes a bit of practice to do it properly. If it is impossible to figure it out, just do it any old way following the instructions as best you can and get along to a spinning group where someone will soon show you what to do.

Some people like to label their carders left and right and old spinning books say that it made them work better if they were always used in the same hand. It makes no discernable difference. You may still come across second-hand carders which have 'left' and 'right' written on them in thick felt tip though.

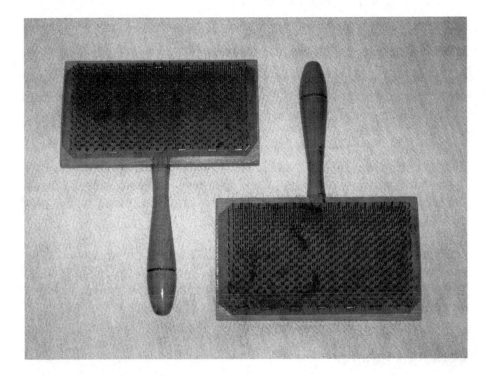

fig 67: hand carders

Another piece of advice that used to be dished out was not to store the two carders with the teeth meshed together. Again it makes no difference so store them however is most convenient for you. What does make a huge difference is making sure you keep them clean.

are the carders in good condition?

If you have inherited a pair of carders with teeth that are either sticky or rusty, buy replacement *card clothing* as it is called. This is available from spinning suppliers and is simple to attach to the carders with either a staple gun or a small hammer and carpet tacks. Do not attempt to scrub the carders clean as not only will the clothing buckle, due to having a rubber front and a fabric backing, but the dampness may remain between the wood and the card clothing causing the teeth to rust and snap off.

New carders have rough edges to the teeth and this makes the wool fibres catch on them. A piece of sandpaper rubbed over the teeth in every direction will improve their performance greatly.

which fibre is suitable for carding?

Carding works best on fibre which is up to 10cm (4in) in length; even very short fibre, as short as 1cm (0.5in) can be carded. As a beginner it is best to save any very short fibre for when you have more experience.

Fibre longer than 10cm (4in) is wider than the carders and it will hang over the front edge. This makes it difficult to deal with and as you card it will try to wrap around the carder teeth and fold back on itself. Longer fibre is therefore better dealt with by combing, which is described in the next section, see page 155.

Any fibre that has a lot of hay seed or other contamination is also better combed, as carding does not remove debris from fibre but combing does. There are mini combs available that can comb fairly short fibres, so this is an option even with fibre that is shorter than 10cm (4in).

carding technique

Carding is the commonest way of preparing fleece and carders are portable and easy to use once you get the hang of the basic technique.

pull out locks of fleece

It is important to keep the staple formation as intact as possible so that the fibre can all be laid on the carders in the same direction. Otherwise some will catch round the teeth and not be carded properly. So hold the fleece in one hand and use the other hand to pull out one lock at a time with a sharp tug. It should come away cleanly, leaving the rest of the fleece tidy.

fig 68: pulling out locks of fleece ready for carding

Sometimes spinners pull out a number of locks in advance and place them in a box or basket. Then you can card without having to keep stopping to pull out more fibre. The carding can also be done in a batch before starting on the spinning. It is a handy thing to take out and about and carding goes quickly whilst chatting to friends. If you card a batch of fibre at once lay the carded *rolags* in a basket or box for future use. Do not do too many at once as they are best spun reasonably fresh. If they are left for too long they would need a re-carding briefly before use because those little hooks on the wool fibres begin to stick together. So don't try spinning two year old rolags.

flick the tips

If you do this before carding, the job is half done. Flicking the tips may be all that is necessary if the fleece is already nice and loose. The idea is to open up the tips of the locks because they are the part that needs the most attention.

If you do not do this, it is likely that some tips will remain stuck together whilst the rest of the fibre is carded. When you come to spin them, the whole lock will come away at once if the tips are not opened out, resulting in a thick lump in the spinning.

fig 69: flicking the tips prior to carding; this is a great shortcut and ensures wool is carded well with minimum effort

To flick the tips, hold an individual lock firmly in one hand by the butt end. You need to hold it firmly enough that the fibre will not pull out of your hand. Sit one of the carders on your thigh, teeth uppermost and hold it with the other hand. Drag the very tip of the lock through the carder teeth to open it up, without carding the rest of the lock. It can help if you press the tip gently into the carder teeth with a finger. The tip should separate into individual fibres and fluff out a little. You are aiming to flick only the very tip of the lock, usually about 0.5-1cm (0.25-0.5in).

lay the locks across one of the carders

We will call the carder you are now going to work with carder A. The other one is carder B. We will call the edge that has the handle on it the **back edge** and the edge opposite the **front edge.**

Remember which hand is holding carder A and which is holding carder B. Write it on the back of your hands as a reminder if necessary but not on the carders.

The carders do not change hands unless you put them down to do something else so this will help to keep track. Which way around you have your hands depends to some extent on whether you are left- or right-handed, but it really does not matter so hold them whichever way feels comfortable.

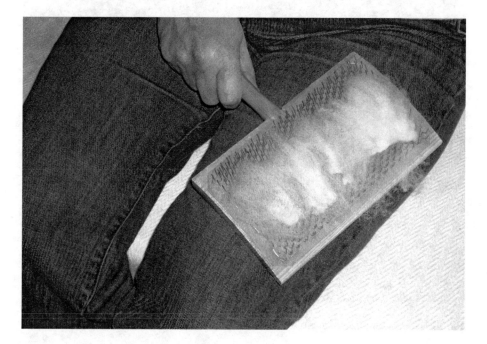

fig 70: locks laid on carder ready for carding

Sit one of the carders (this will be carder A) across your thigh with the teeth uppermost as you did when flicking the tips of the locks. The handle should be towards the inside of the leg. If the left hand is holding the handle, the carder should be on the right leg and vice versa.

Lay four to six locks, with their tips already flicked, across the carder from front to back. (That is the narrowest way, from the handle to the front edge.) The locks should lie fully on the carders with no fibre hanging over the edges.

Resist the temptation to add more locks as they will fluff up a lot when you card them. If you put too much fibre on the carders at one time the carder teeth will not penetrate it and no matter how hard you try the fibre will not all get carded.

This means starting out with what looks like *too little* fibre on the carders.

begin carding the fibre

Leave carder A where it is, on your thigh with the teeth facing upwards. Restrain it by holding the handle.

fig 71: begin carding the fibre

Pick up the second carder (carder B) holding it as if it was a hairbrush with the teeth facing downwards. Stroke carder B over carder A but do not mesh the teeth. The carding happens in the space between the carders. If you can hear a grating sound you are meshing the teeth and need to hold the carders further apart.

You should find that this is a gentle action, not one that needs a great deal of force. You cannot deal with matted or felted fibre by carding – you will just tear the fibre apart and it will take a great deal of effort whilst yielding poor results. Carding is meant to separate the fibres of a good quality fleece. Stroke carder B over carder A four or five times. Some of the fibre will transfer from carder A to carder B.

transfer the fibre

The next step is to transfer all of the remaining fibre from carder A to carder B. This is a bit tricky to explain and when you first hear it described or even see it done, it can seem impossible to understand. If you cannot get it to work, simply remove the fibre by hand and if it needs more carding replace it on the carders and do it some more. It will still work reasonably well but won't look as elegant!

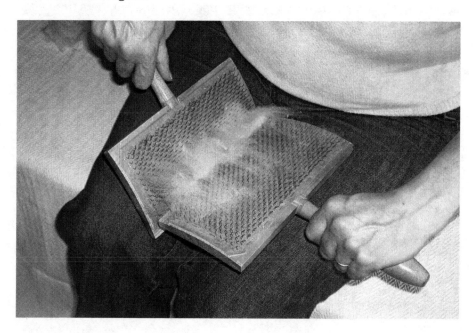

fig 72: transfer the fibre

Turn carder B (which is the carder on the top at this point) so that the teeth face upwards. Do this without changing your grip on the carder if you can. Move it so that the front of the carder faces away from you rather than side on; this will let you turn it over and help.

Lay carder A on top of carder B also with the teeth facing upwards and with the front edge of carder A right up by the handle of carder B. Now tilt both carders so that there is a 90° degree gap between them. Lift what was the top carder upwards and the fibre should transfer to it.

Turn it back over again without changing your grip. Now continue to card with the carders in the same position as at the beginning, only this time you are starting with the fibre on the top carder.

Then repeat the transfer instructions to get all the fibre back onto one carder. You are then ready to take the fibre off the carders, or **doff** it.

doff the fibre

Doffing the fibre means taking it off the carders and is a bit like transferring it from one carder to the other but also a bit different. You turn carder B over so that both carders have the teeth uppermost and put them front edge to front edge: that is the edge opposite the handle.

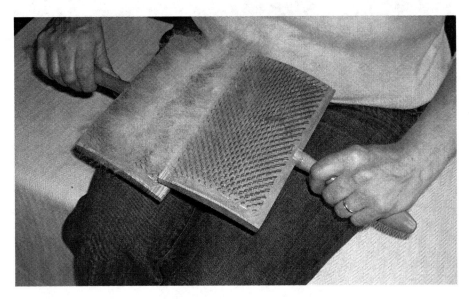

fig 73. doffing or removing the carded fibre from the carders

Do this without changing grip. By now you probably feel like a contortionist but it really is possible. As before, turn carder B to face away from you rather than side on before trying to turn it over.

Then tilt both carders slightly so that the front teeth mesh together and lift the empty one followed by the full one. This will lift the fibre free of the carders. It can then be used as it is (called a **carded batt**) or laid onto one of the carders and gently rolled into a sausage shape (called a **rolag**).

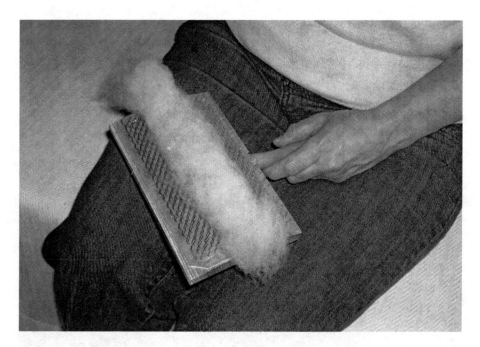

fig 74: finished rolag

The carders can be cleaned of any remaining fibre once all the carding is finished. Do this by using one carder to lift the fibre out of the other, or use a dog comb. It is easy to forget to do this when you start carding again and leaving it could result in leftover white fibres appearing in a brown fleece when they are used next time.

combing the fibre

Most spinners start out by buying a set of carders and learn to use them first. You do not need combs as well but a fair number of people find them useful and really enjoy using them.

Combs produce smoother yarns and are good for fibre that is too long for carders. Some people do not like using carders at all yet are quite happy to comb fibre. Combing is a good option if fibre contains a lot of debris as the debris can be combed out.

Carders, on the other hand, produce fibre that is easier to spin and makes warmer, fluffier yarns with more stretch and give, so there are pros and cons to both methods.

There are three main types of combs available: Mini combs, Viking combs and English Wool combs. Combing can also be done using a dog comb. Some spinning suppliers make their own combs and there are variations on the three basic types.

The fibre needs to be a minimum of about 7.5cm (3in) long for mini combs, 10cm (4in) for the larger Viking combs and about 10cm (4in) for English wool combs. This is only a rough guide and, if you are not sure, try it and see if it works.

using a dog comb

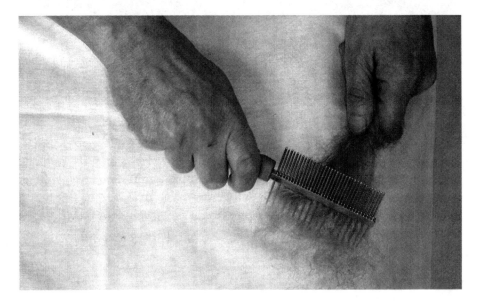

fig 75: combing fibre with a dog comb

The simplest and cheapest way to comb fibre is to use a metal-toothed dog comb. It is slower than purpose-made combs and can get a bit tedious if you are processing a lot of fibre, or if the fibre is very long. For the odd project a dog comb is sufficient but if you comb a lot of fibre a set of combs made specifically for spinners is very worthwhile.

To use a dog comb, hold the fibre very firmly in one hand. If it is long enough wrap it around a finger to stop it from pulling away. Start combing from the tips and work gradually up the fibres towards your fingers. The fibre is ready when all of the fibres are separated and tidy.

Large or medium purpose-made combs can be used for fibre that is too long for carders. Examples would be mohair, Wenslydale or Lincoln Longwool. These can also be processed using a flick carder and instructions for this are in the section on spinning mohair, see page 172.

mini combs

fig 76: Louet mini combs are great for shorter, delicate fibre such as fine Shetland or Merino

Small combs can be used for shorter, more delicate fibre when you want a smooth yarn. Very delicate fibre can be damaged by carding, and it causes **nepps** (little bobbles) in some fine fibre, so mini combs are a good alternative. The nepps are caused by single fibres being stretched between two carder teeth, then pinging off and coiling up like little springs. So if the fibre gets worse the more you card it, try combing instead.

Mini combs are not suitable for longer fibres which will damage them. I frequently use them to prepare small rovings for fine spinning.

Louet make sets of mini combs with single or double rows of teeth. The single ones are less prone to getting stuck on snags and it is easier to draw the fibre off them. Other manufacturers make similar combs so have a look around and compare prices. The plastic insert holding the teeth on mini combs sometimes comes out but is it simple to glue it back in.

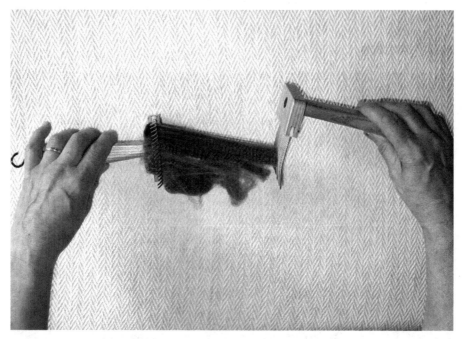

fig 77: using hand-held Louet mini combs; start at the tips of the fibre and work up: hold the combs at right angles to each other when possible

Spinners often buy mini combs in a flush of enthusiasm and mini combs seem to appear second-hand more often than the other kinds. They are much cheaper than the Viking or English combs and I suspect people sometimes buy them hoping that they will be suitable for a greater range of tasks than they actually are.

Viking combs

Viking combs can cope with a large range of fibres. They are good multi-purpose combs: cheaper, lighter and easier to use than English wool combs yet more robust than Louet mini combs. They usually have two rows of teeth but different makes vary.

fig 78: Valkyrie Viking combs with pad to hold one comb whilst combing

Some sets are hand held and some have an optional stand. The stand is very useful but not essential. I have two-row Valkyrie Viking combs and use them for many different fibres and for blending. There is no need to buy a set each of English wool combs and Viking combs – choose one or the other. Two row or *pitch* means the combs have a double row of **tines** or teeth on them. Majacraft mini combs deserve a mention here. Although they are small, the teeth are strong. Unlike Louet mini combs, which are great for more delicate fibres, the Majacraft combs are suitable for combing longer fibre and are a great portable and compact tool for wool combing.

fig 79: Majacraft mini combs are robust with strong tines and suitable for stronger, longer fibres such as Wensleydale

English wool combs

The larger traditional English wool combs are four row (**pitch**) combs with very sharp points. They are heavier to use than other combs and expensive to buy but real workhorses. If you want to do traditional **worsted** spinning with longer wool they are great. They produce a lot of combed fibre quickly and will process fibre faster than the Viking combs because of their size and robustness. I find the Viking combs easier to use and more versatile. They are also much more portable than the English wool combs.

fig 80: four pitch English wool combs

My Guild has a set that members can borrow and they are useful for the occasional time we want to use them. One member has become keen on them and now has her own set which she uses frequently.

how to use Viking and English wool combs

washing and preparing the fibre

Traditionally, when using English wool combs, the wool is hot washed to remove all grease and then sprinkled or sprayed with a mixture of oil and water (olive oil works well). I find that cold-soaked fleece works well with any combs and it is not always necessary to add both oil and water – sometimes spraying the wool with water is enough. Oil and water helps a lot on hot-washed fleece, which can fluff up too much and be harder to comb without it. Experiment and see what works for you. Make sure there is an old towel under the fibre if you are adding oil, as it may otherwise roll off onto the floor.

load the combs

Combs are sharp so take care, especially when loading them with fleece and make sure the cover is on if they are left unattended.

If there is a stand for the combs, clamp this to a heavy table or other surface. A window sill works well because it does not move.

Pull out locks of fibre as described in the section on carding, see page 148. There is no need to flick the tips of the locks prior to combing.

Put three to five rows of locks onto one comb. If you are using English wool combs you can put more on because the combs have longer tines. Aim to load the combs about half full.

Fix the locks on by holding one end in each hand. Spear the butt end of the fibre, allowing a small amount of the butt of the lock to protrude behind the tines and with the rest of the lock hanging down from the front of the comb.

If one of the combs is fixed onto a stand, load this one. Push the locks all the way down the comb but then slide them up again a little when you are ready to comb the fibre.

comb the fibre

fig 81: work with combs at right angles

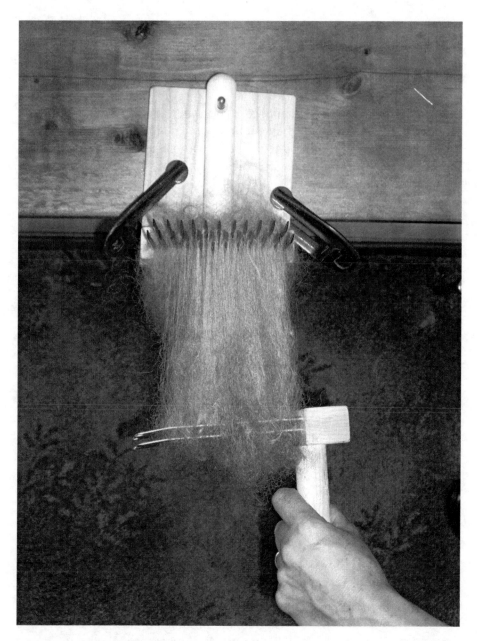

fig 82: combing the fibre

If you are using two hand-held combs, hold one in each hand. If the loaded comb is on a stand, hold the free comb. If using English wool combs, hold the free comb with both hands, as they are heavy. It is essential to use the stand with English wool combs.

The aim is to have the combs at right angles to each other at all times when combing. So if one comb has the tines facing upright, the other one will have them facing sideways. With English wool combs the fixed comb is loaded whilst facing upright then turned onto its side before combing commences.

Start from the tip of the fibre and work your way along it. Comb the fibre so that the ends separate and then continue until all the fibre is combed and quite a lot of it has transferred to the other comb. If it is hard to comb, slide the fibre a little further up the comb and work your way in from the tip of the locks more slowly.

change direction

Once most of the fibre has transferred to the other comb, the fibre may be ready. If it needs more combing, transfer it back again.

For the second pass on English Wool Combs, the hand-held comb is held in the same position and is taken towards the fixed one so that the tines on the fixed comb bite into the fibre. The combs are always held at right angles to each other and the fixed comb is always on its side whilst the combing takes place, being turned upright only to load and unload the combs.

If using Viking combs, hold the hands so that the combs are still at right angles to each other. Instead of the free comb combing the tip of the fibre on the fixed comb, lift the free comb up above the fixed one and bring it downwards so that the tip of the fibre catches onto the upright fixed comb tines. Work up the fibre as before. Use hand-held combs in a similar way and read 'upright comb' for 'fixed comb'.

If you cannot work the instructions out, just try it. Do it as best you can and it will still comb the fibre.

draw the fibre off the combs

The fibre is then drawn off the combs so as to make a long roving ready to spin. This is similar to pre-drafting. Remind yourself of how to pre-draft, see page 66, before starting to pull the wool off the combs if necessary.

As with pre-drafting and drafting, it is vital that your hands are further apart than the length of the fibre or it will not pull apart, so check the fibre length.

fig 83: drawing the fibre off the combs

Slide the fibre up from the base of the combs slightly before you start as this makes it easier to draw it off. Some people use a small object with a hole in it called a *diz* which helps to get the roving even, but you do not need to. A metal washer, a smooth piece of wood with a hole drilled in it or a limpet shell with a hole in the middle can all be used as a diz.

Stroke the fibre to a point before you start and if the comb is on a stand, make sure it is clamped firmly to a table or window sill and draw the fibre off hand over hand. If hand held, hold the comb firmly in one hand and draw the fibre off with the other one. Pull a length of fibre off then let go of the fibre completely before grasping it again further along and pulling some more. This is similar to pre-drafting and the hands should not slide along the fibre or all the good work will be undone.

As with pre-drafting it is important to draft only half of the fibre length at a time or the roving will become thin.

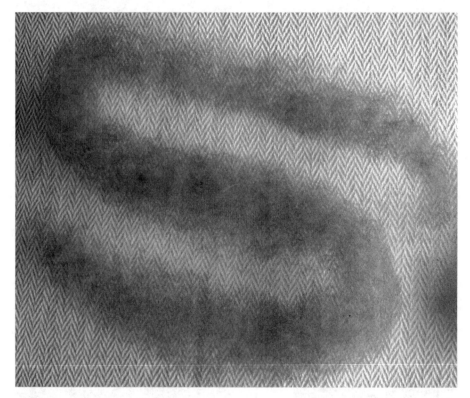

fig 84: combed fibre ready to spin

If you are using a diz, slide it onto the fibre beforehand and push it up firmly against the fibre. Draw the fibre off the combs as before except that it goes through the diz. Pull off a small length of fibre, then push the diz up firmly again and keep doing that until most of the fibre is drawn off.

discard what is left

There is always a little bit of fibre left on the combs and this consists of fibres that are too short to be drawn off. Any debris will also be in this leftover fibre and it should therefore be discarded.

spinning fibres other than wool

Most spinners – with the exception of vegan spinners – start by learning to spin wool. It is the best fibre to learn on because of those little hooks on the individual fibres, which hold the wool together until it is safely spun and on the bobbin.

As already discussed, the best way to improve your skill is to spin small amounts of as many different kinds of wool as possible rather than trying to finish one fleece. Wool spun from fleece will be quite different to the same wool spun from a combed top so try both.

The next step is to experiment with fibres other than wool but it is important to start with the right ones.

I have mentioned them in the order that I recommend you try spinning them – Alpaca, mohair, then silk, then some other animal fibres and finally synthetic fibres such as soya, viscose, milk protein and seaweed. There is no firm rule about this and there are some in the synthetics section that are quite easy to spin and some in the silk section that are tricky, so feel free to try fibres from any section. Alpaca is a good place to start though, assuming you have the right quality of fibre.

if you struggle, blend it

If any fibre is hard to spin, blend a small amount with some nice, medium-staple wool. Use carders to do this and start with about 10% of the new fibre. Make two rolags and spin them.

Make a couple more, this time with a little bit more of the new fibre and a little bit less wool in them. Do not change the amount suddenly, but build it up gradually by adding a little more each time and spinning the batts as you go. It is best to blend a couple and then spin them rather than to blend a whole series of batts at once. That way you can adjust the quantity of the new fibre depending on how you get on. If you struggle, back up and add a bit less. Blending like this also makes the fibre easier to join on.

If you decide not to spin the fibre in its pure form at the moment, that's fine too. You will create some wonderful blended yarns and these are actually the ones that knitters pay a premium for. There is no need to stop at blending two fibres either, a third one can be added in and blending fibres and colours is a whole new area to explore.

joining on

Other fibres can be a little harder to join on than wool is, because they do not have those little hooks on the fibres that make wool so user-friendly. Use a handspun singles leader on the bobbin as opposed to a commercial yarn if possible.

When emptying bobbins, resist the urge to tidy up and leave any leftover bits of yarn on the bobbins for future use. Whatever method you are using, do a longer join than usual and add plenty of twist to make sure it does not come apart.

If you are working on a high top spindle, pull some fibre off and put this through the hook of the spindle just like we did with woollen fibre. Twist the spindle by hand until there is some twist in the fibre, pulling the fibre out as you go so that the yarn gets longer. Then take if off the hook and tie it directly onto the shaft of the spindle. With fibres other than wool it is much easier to do this than to join it onto yarn that is already on the spindle.

On a spinning wheel, make sure there is plenty of twist built up behind your fingers before joining the new fibre on. Do a nice long join and let the twist through to secure it firmly. Add some more twist and get the join onto the bobbin as soon as possible.

If you cannot get a join using the methods above, using either a wheel or a spindle, tie a loop in the leader yarn and thread the fibre through it as described in the *emergency measures* section, page 78. This works on both a spinning wheel and a hand spindle.

alpaca

Alpaca is not stretchy like wool and lacks both the hooks on the fibres and the grease that wool has. This makes it a little slipperier to spin but it is an ideal fibre to progress to once you have some confidence with wool.

There is no need for months of practice before trying Alpaca though and when I teach beginners to spin at a local Alpaca centre, we spin Alpaca in the afternoon. It will take longer if you are teaching yourself, but half the battle is getting good Alpaca fibre to learn on.

Alpaca varies greatly in softness and length – the fibre from a baby Alpaca can be 5cm (3in) long, whilst Suri Alpaca (a particular variety that is long and curly) can be 30cm (12 in) long. Alpaca can be bought as fleece or tops and fleece is easier to start with.

What you are looking for is a fine fleece with fibres that are about 10-15cm (4-6in) long that hang together in a mass of loose fibre rather than being in individual staples or clumps. It should be relatively free from debris. Look carefully for debris as Alpacas love to roll.

Alpaca farmers do not always know what spinners are looking for – and indeed many spinners are not sure what to look for either so it is important to explain what you want.

how to spin alpaca

Alpaca fibre as described above can be spun without carding, washing or other preparation and no special techniques are needed. Just spin it straight from a handful of fleece using some of the techniques you have learned about controlling the twist.

Do not to put too much twist in it, as this makes the yarn hard. Practise with more twist to start with and then reduce the amount once you have confidence with the fibre. The yarn with the most pleasing appearance will be harder to the touch than that which looks a little under spun so experiment and bear the intended use in mind.

mohair

Mohair is long, curly fibre that looks similar to Wensleydale and other Longwools. It is not wool at all, but fibre from the Angora goat. Angora itself is produced solely by Angora rabbits.

Mohair is a smooth shiny fibre and the fluffy mohair yarn that we are used to seeing in the shops is actually spun as a smooth but loopy yarn. The loops are then cut and the yarn is brushed to obtain the familiar fuzz.

Handspun mohair is delightful and not at all itchy – very different to its commercial counterpart, although there are a handful of specialist suppliers who sell smooth mohair yarns.

Kid mohair is beautifully soft and much shorter in length than the adult fibre. It can be used for the softest baby wear. As well as being longer, adult mohair has thicker fibres. Because it is also smooth and shiny it produces a nice but hard-wearing yarn providing it is not spun with too much twist, which can turn it into something resembling steel cable.

Mohair is often used for handspun socks due to its hard wearing qualities but is a versatile fibre. The best way to get hold of it is to find a local breeders' society, as small owners do not always have a good market for their fibre. Like Longwools, mohair has heavy grease in it and needs to be hot washed before use.

how to spin mohair

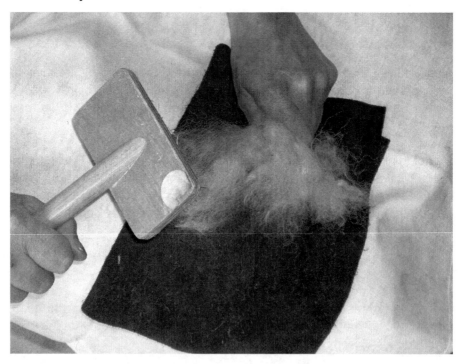

fig 85: using a flick carder

Adult mohair is best combed rather than carded because of the length of the fibre. It is quite hard work with a dog comb but it can be done. If you do not have wool combs another option is to use a flick carder. This is small, single carder that is used with a piece of leather.

To use a flick carder, lay the piece of leather or other protection on your thigh. Pull off an individual lock of fibre and hold it firmly by the butt end. Wrap the fibre around a finger to hold it more firmly if possible. Rather than combing, **hit and lift** the carder, working up from the tips of the fibre. Then turn the lock around and flick the other end.

Spin it with a light twist for a soft yarn and more twist for hard-wearing rug yarns.

using mohair without spinning

Mohair can be used without being spun at all. To use it in knitting, crochet or weaving, pull out individual washed locks – hand-dyed ones are very effective – and just knit or weave them into your project randomly to add texture and colour.

It can also be used on a **peg loom** – a very simple weaving loom used to make rugs, wall hangings and cushion covers with very thick yarn or unspun fleece.

Mohair and Longwools tend to work much better on peg looms than on other kinds of fleece because they keep their shape and do not go bobbly.

spinning silk

Silk prepared in certain ways is ideal to start with, being relatively easy to spin. Some preparations of silk are harder to spin though, so it is important to know the difference.

As well as being spun on its own, silk can make lovely knitting yarns when it is plyed or blended with wool, Alpaca or other fibres. Similar yarns are very expensive to buy but relatively easy to spin.

choose the right silk for the job

All of the silk preparations mentioned are easy to get hold of from specialist spinning suppliers, but do compare prices as they vary a lot.

Cocoons, hankies and silk caps produce fine yarns that are relatively easy to spin and seldom break during spinning. They make it easier to spin a fine silk yarn, which can be a challenge using silk tops. On the other hand, if you want a completely smooth, shiny yarn that is not quite so fine, then choose silk tops. Throwsters waste, pulled silk waste and sari silk are preparations that give a lot of texture and are usually blended with other fibres.

silk cocoons

Silk cocoons are actually very easy to spin. Silk fibres are long and because the fibre in cocoons has not been cut, it tends not to break whilst being spun. The cocoon fibre is not very slippery which also helps.

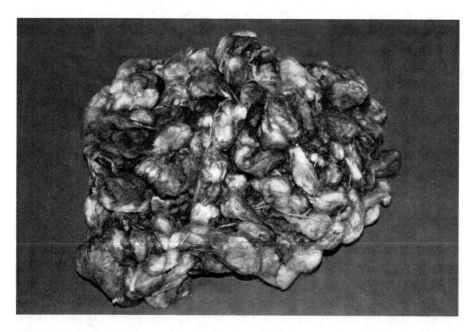

fig 86: de-gummed and dyed silk cocoons; these can be spun one at a time without further preparation

Purchase de-gummed cocoons for spinning. You can de-gum them yourself but buying them de-gummed is a good way to start. They will come as a mass of individual cocoons but joined together by some fibres that have unwound from the cocoons. Pull one cocoon away from the mass with a sharp tug.

Then work only with this individual cocoon. Do not be tempted to try and spin more than one cocoon at a time as they will become tangled and hard to draft.

silk hankies and caps – stretched out cocoons

The fibres in both hankies and caps are also very long. The hankies or caps are made up of individual cocoons stretched out in layers over a form. In the case of a hanky this is a square hanky-sized frame and for caps the form is larger and dome-shaped.

Silk worms spin a filament that continues throughout the whole cocoon, starting at the outside and finishing in the centre. As they get to the centre, the quality is not so good because they begin to run out of silk.

The final layer is therefore made up of short, papery fibres and is called the *basinette*. This gives silk yarn spun from hankies and caps (and from the cocoons themselves) a slight texture with tiny papery flecks every so often. There are some breaks in the fibre, where the silk grub hatched or the cocoon was cut as part of processing, but the fibres remain very long.

Applying some hand cream before working with silk caps and hankies can make it easier to work with them, as the fibres tend to catch on your fingers – although eventually you get the knack of how to wiggle your fingers as you work and the hand cream is no longer necessary.

hankies

There is a lot less silk in a hanky than there is in a silk cap and because of this they can work out more expensive but some people find them easier to work with than caps.

To prepare hankies for spinning, grasp the hanky firmly in the middle with one hand and pull away just a thin layer, also from the middle, with the other.

Pull this thin layer sharply away from the rest of the hanky and then pre-draft it.

Because the fibres are very long, work with your hands at least 30cm (12in) apart. The fibres are unlikely to come apart altogether because of their length and can in fact be used for knitting without spinning them at all, for details see page 177.

The length of the fibres makes them hard to draft so pre-drafting them properly is very important. The pre-drafting is done in the same way as it was with wool tops, so please see page 66 if necessary. The most important thing is to have your hands a lot further apart than when working with wool and it helps if, when both pre-drafting and drafting, the fibre is fanned sideways with the fingers to create a wide drafting triangle.

As you pre-draft, just let the long roving fall to the floor beside you. Aim to do most of the drafting before you start to spin. To see how thin the yarn will be once it is spun, twist some between the fingers. You may be surprised by just how much thinner it gets.

The pre-drafted roving can be rolled up and kept for spinning later if desired. It is not necessary to wind it around a knitting needle or the inside of a toilet roll, as is sometimes suggested. It will stay tidy if simply wound around your hand and then kept in a box or bag until needed. Winding anything into a ball actually inserts a small amount of twist and this is enough to stop the roving from sticking together.

silk caps or 'bells'

A silk cap is a thick, bell-shaped hat of fibre which consists of many layers of cocoons stretched over a bell-shaped mould. There is a lot more silk in a cap than there is in a hanky. A whole bundle of caps is called a **bell** but the two words are sometimes used interchangeably.

The only thing that is trickier with caps than hankies is getting a layer off the main fibre mass. So long as you get a thin enough layer it is plain sailing from then on. Pulling off a really thin layer is more important with a cap than with a hanky because there is so much more fibre on a cap. If you pull off too much, you could be working with the equivalent of a whole hanky at once.

fig 87: silk cap

To pull off a thin layer, put one hand right inside the cap and grip the fibre firmly from the inside. With the other hand, pull up a thin layer at the top (crown) of the cap from the outside. Grip this firmly then give three sharp tugs as you pull your hands apart. This should be enough to separate the layer completely from the rest of the cap, but if not just tug it some more. It is important to tug sharply or the rest of the cap will lose its shape and drag extra fibre away along with the thinner layer.

Pre-draft the layer until it separates and becomes one long length rather than a circle. Then continue to pre-draft until it is the thickness you want, as with the silk hankies.

Fanning out the fibre to create a larger drafting triangle is even more important with caps than with hankies and you should draft all of the fibre before spinning. If the fibre will not draft, there is either too much silk to work with at one time, or your hands need to be even further apart.

knitting with unspun silk hankies and caps

A little known fact about silk caps and hankies is that you can knit with them without really spinning them at all. The fibres are so long that they do not need twist to prevent the yarn from breaking, only to make it neat and tidy.

Follow the directions on how to spin caps and hankies, see page 175, as far as the pre-drafting stage so that you have a long roving of unspun silk. Make sure the roving is nice and chunky, as it will otherwise disappear to nothing and be too fine to knit with.

Now it is **thigh rolled** to stick the fibres together a bit and make a nicer yarn. Roll a 30cm (12in) length on your thigh. It helps to use some hand cream or wet the palm of the hand periodically.

For the next length, roll in the opposite direction. All you are doing is helping the fibres to stick together a bit to keep them tidy, so the direction of the twist does not actually matter. Going in alternate directions avoids getting a tangle at the other end of the roving.

Roll the twisted roving up into a ball and do another. It is good to make a few rovings at once, as they are more likely to be a similar thickness.

Silk is a lovely, warm fibre and these rovings make nice mittens, hats and scarves. They are also great in textured crochet or weaving.

silk tops

Silk tops consist of fibres that have been cut to length and then combed. Combing removes any shorter fibres and aligns those that remain so that they are all going in the same direction. That and the smoothness of the fibres makes them challenging to spin with.

Spinners who are new to silk sometimes try Bombyx mori (white) silk tops first and are put off. This is the hardest silk preparation to work with, so try spinning cocoons first if you have not done so already. Then graduate to hankies, caps and finally to tops.

Silk tops can be hard to get even and there are often thick and thin parts. This is where the tops have been drafted too far, meaning you get to the end of too many fibres at one time just as with any tops. The silk from tops comes away all of a sudden though, making this a bigger problem.

the solution - start with tussah silk

There are two main types of silk tops available to spinners, which come from different varieties of silk worms; they are Tussah and Bombyx mori. There are a number of other varieties of silk worms including one that is native to the United Kingdom but the other varieties do not produce much silk and are not readily available on a commercial basis. The UK's indigenous silk worm produces a tiny amount of silk but it is still a silk worm.

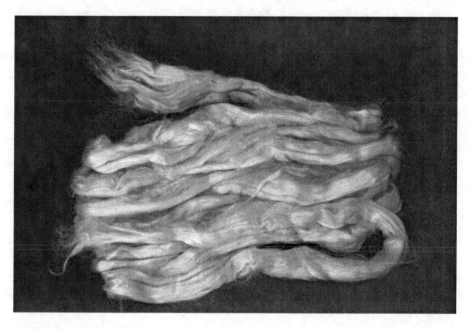

fig 88: Tussah silk tops

Tussah silk is a natural creamy beige colour and is sometimes called wild silk, although it is cultivated. The difference in colour between it and Bombyx mori (depending on what you read) is thought to be partly due to a diet higher in tannins and partly due to the nature of the silk worm itself.

The fibres in Tussah silk are not as smooth and shiny as those in Bombyx mori (known as B. mori for short) and this makes it easier to spin.

join it carefully

Because even Tussah silk tops are slippery, take extra care when joining it on. Follow the directions for joining as described in the section on spinning cocoons, see page 174. If you just cannot get it to stay joined to the yarn on the bobbin, make a loop at the end of the leader yarn, thread the fibre through it and double it back on itself as described previously. This technique can be used for any tricky join.

spin from the fold or over the finger

Spinning from the fold, or over the finger, means that the fibres are no longer all facing in the same direction. This makes it easier to spin as the yarn does not keep coming apart. These techniques are particularly useful when spinning silk tops, either on a wheel or hand spindle, because the fibres in silk tops are slippery and otherwise want to come away all at once. Fan the fibres out as you spin them as well.

If you do struggle to spin Tussah tops, blend a small amount of Tussah with medium-length wool using carders and build up the quantity of silk in the blends just like we did with the Alpaca, see page 169.

In theory silk tops can be carded on their own to make a rolag or batt, but in reality the fibre tends to come apart when you remove it from the carders. Even a tiny bit of wool makes a huge difference.

With even a little bit of practice you should find working with silk gets easier. If not, then just continue to spin it blended with wool and do not lose any sleep over it.

Bombyx mori (B. mori) silk tops

B. mori is white silk which is smoother and shinier than Tussah. Once you have got the hang of spinning Tussah silk, spinning B. mori will be less of a challenge, so make sure you try some Tussah first.

B. mori comes either in the form of a silk top like the Tussah silk or in what is called a *silk brick*. This is actually a very wide top – usually about 15cm (6in) wide and is called a brick because of the way it is folded up. (Tussah silk is not often available as a brick.) Silk bricks come in two qualities – B2 and A1.

fig 89: B. mori silk tops

B2 is the lower quality and usually cheaper. It has been combed fewer times and still has more of the shorter, fuzzy fibres in it than A1 quality tops. Although it is theoretically lower quality, B2 tops are easier to spin and the results are every bit as pleasing as using A1 quality.

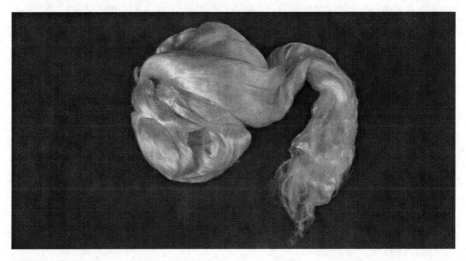

fig 90: B. mori silk brick;. a brick is a very wide top that has been combed fewer times

If using a silk brick, pull off a length that is about the width of a normal combed wool top and then treat it just as you would any other combed top. Spin the tops from the fold or over the finger for best results rather than from a pencil roving.

If you struggle to spin B. mori silk on its own, start with a blend as suggested for Tussah silk, see page 180.

throwsters waste

Throwsters waste is a mass of fine, shiny threads. They are the waste left over when silk is reeled direct from cocoons but sometimes also contain some loom waste. Because throwsters waste is reeled from cocoons, it still has sericin in it, the gum the silk worm uses to glue the cocoon together. (Incidentally, sericin is used for all sorts of things, including as an additive in skin and hair care products.)

Although you can de-gum silk waste, most people choose to buy it already de-gummed and that is certainly the best way when you are starting.

Many of the threads in throwsters waste are very long and they can be quite tangled. Because of this, it can be a challenge to spin it on its own and the results are not especially pleasing or useful, although it can look lovely used in small quantities as a textured accent in textiles. It can also be used as a textured yarn in knitting, weaving and crochet without being spun first.

Blended with other fibres such as wool or Alpaca it will give a beautiful textured yarn and the shine of the silk contrasts well with the wool.

To do this, chop it into 2.5-5cm (1-2in) lengths and blend it using carders. Aim for a subtle effect and 5-10% of throwsters waste is plenty. Used as a singles or unplyed yarn the colour and texture shows up well. Another possibility is to ply it with a single of fine silk spun from a silk cap, hankies or cocoons, or with a plain, commercially-spun fine yarn. Cones of fine yarn can often be picked up in charity shops or from other spinners or weavers.

pulled silk waste

Pulled silk waste is another waste silk, but is short and fuzzy as opposed to long and shiny – usually 2.5-5cm (1-2in) long. It is multi-coloured and looks good carded in with other fibres such as wool or Alpaca. Used along with a naturally coloured fleece, the colours are very effective. As with throwsters, only a small quantity is needed to be effective. Spun on its own the multi-coloured threads blend together and create a muddy effect which looks a bit like you have spun the contents of the vacuum cleaner bag.

sari silk

This consists of multi-coloured loom waste. The colours vary so do check. It can be spun on its own and bought as yarn. It tends to be a rather hard, stiff yarn though. An alternative is to spin it yourself with less twist or to cut it and blend it like throwsters waste.

how to de-gum silk

Dissolve 2 tablespoons of washing soda and 2 teaspoons of washing up liquid or laundry detergent in warm water in a large cooking pot that is not used to cook food, or a dye bucket.

Put the silk in and bring it gently to a slow simmer and heat for 20 minutes. Drain and repeat, this time simmering for 10 minutes. Rinse, put it in an old pillow case or net bag and spin dry.

angora

Angora is produced only by Angora rabbits and not by Angora goats, which produce mohair. Cashmere, on the other hand, is produced by both Cashmere goats and rabbits!

Handspun Angora does not shed like its commercial counterpart and is a completely smooth yarn when it is first made. The halo of fluff appears over a week or so once the garment is in use as the tips of the smooth fibres gradually work their way out. Unlike the very short fibres in commercial Angora, these do not come out altogether and I have a fifteen-year-old shawl with a handspun Angora border that has never shed a single fibre.

The fibre can be bought from breeders so contact the breed society. There is often someone in spinning groups or Guilds who keeps rabbits.

how to spin angora

Angora spun on its own is extremely warm and very fluffy. It is usually either blended or plyed with another fibre such as wool or silk. Silk is ideal for this as the shiny silk compliments the fluffy Angora. A small amount of Angora in a blend gives a lot of fluff so 10-20% is plenty.

Another option is to use 100% Angora in a project but only every so often. I knitted a lovely cardigan with Shetland and Angora doing this and put two rows of angora in for every twelve of Shetland.

Spin Angora with lots of twist and use the fastest whorl on the spinning wheel. Do take a sample off the wheel and double it back on itself for reference when plying the yarn later as it is easy to under-ply.

When knitting with angora use knitting needles at least two sizes larger than you think you could possibly need because as the fibre fluffs up it fills in the spaces between the stitches. If you do not, it will end up like a solid mat. Knit a sample and keep it in your pocket for a week to make sure.

rabbits make great fibre pets

If you want to own a fibre animal an Angora rabbit is a great choice as they are especially friendly rabbits and can be kept in an ordinary house and garden. There are breed societies in most countries and this is the place to start. Incredibly, one Angora rabbit will produce as much fibre in a year as a sheep, but spread out over the year rather than all at the same time. Having kept one I can confirm that this is true and was glad I only had one rabbit. Cashmere rabbits produce a tiny amount of fibre by comparison.

camel and other luxury animal fibres (with hair in them)

Fibres with guard hairs include Camel, Llama, Cashmere and Musk ox (or Qiviut). Alpaca does not have guard hairs even though Llama does.

Most of these fibres are available de-haired and ready to spin as tops or carded fibre, which is a better bet than buying fleece with the hair still in it. A fleece can seem like a bargain until you start removing the hairs and there are always a lot more than it seems. It is possible to get lucky and find fibre with only a few hairs in it. Check carefully and take any fibre out of its bag before purchasing as the best may be on top.

Cashmere goat fibre needs de-hairing but Cashmere rabbit fibre does not so this is another useful bunny fibre if you do not need much of it.

camel

Camel fibre in its raw state consists of a soft, downy layer – the bit that spinners want – and guard hairs, the bit spinners don't want unless they are spinning for rugs.

Camel down – or baby Camel down – is readily available and a good fibre in this group to start with. It is longer than Cashmere and many other luxury fibres and not too slippery, making it relatively easy to spin. The colour varies from pale to quite dark beige.

Camel and other luxury fibres are often available blended with silk and although these blends are nice they are expensive. It is simple to blend the fibres yourself using carders and the results are cheaper and often better.

musk ox or qiviut

Musk ox is quite straightforward to spin so long as you give it plenty of twist and providing the fibre is a decent length. Check this because the length can vary quite a bit.

It usually comes as a mass of fibre and does not need carding. It is two coloured, with light, creamy colours and a darker brown. If it has been commercially processed the colour will be homogenous.

The fibre is from a great big beast that lives in the very cold climate of the Arctic. It is some of the warmest fibre available and I once read that it is the only animal that sits out arctic snowstorms rather than seeking cover. Given that most of us have central heating, it is a challenge to wear a garment made from 100% Musk ox unless you live in an extremely cold area.

Blend it or ply it with a cooler fibre such as silk. Use knitting needles at least 2 sizes larger than usual, knit a swatch just like you would with Angora and keep this in a pocket for a week to see how much it fluffs up.

yak, bison and cashmere

Yak and Bison fibres are short and a dense dark brown colour with little lustre, although Yak is occasionally available in white. Cashmere comes in a range of shades and is seen as the all time luxury fibre.

Buy all of these fibres de-haired and ready to spin. They do not need carding but can be challenging and slow to spin in the normal sense of the word unless you use extended or long-draw techniques because the fibres are so short.

Long draw from very small rolags or **punis** is the traditional way to spin them on a treadle spinning wheel but not many spinners are actually proficient in long draw or English long draw these days and it is often confused with extended draw which is a slightly different technique.

Check the fibre length when purchasing, as some is considerably longer than others, which can be an advantage. Short fibres can be spun on a charkha and if you know how to use one it is the fastest way to spin them.

Long draw, extended draw and spinning with a charkha are topics for another book and there is not the space to go into them properly here.

Another great way to spin short, luxury fibres for a lovely light yarn is to use a technique called **trapping**.

Use two cones of fine yarn and place one on either side of you. Attach both strands to the bobbin core and hold them together so that they go over your index finger with a small gap between them. Now tuck a small amount of the fibre under the two strands but on top of the finger along with the yarns and spin it all together. Run the finger back so that the fibre goes evenly in between the yarns.

This sounds tricky but is not too hard to get the hang of. As the twist goes into the yarns the fibre is trapped evenly between them.

Once you have spun it, this yarn should be plyed with another strand of the fine yarn to make sure the fibre is secure. It creates a light, airy yarn that is often nicer than the same fibres spun in a more traditional way.

the hair of the dog – spinning pet fur

Hair from certain dogs and long-haired cats is similar to some of the luxury fibres described above. Any pet fibre that is soft and not full of guard hairs is suitable. Samoyed and Husky are the commonest dog fibres used for spinning. The undercoat of many dogs such as German Shepherds is nice and soft. Spinners fall into two camps, those who love to spin pet fur and those who hate it. The smell can be off-putting but the intensity of the smell seems to vary from animal to animal.

The fibre is very warm so ply it with another fibre or blend it. Follow the instructions for Angora, see page 184, as this fibre also has a halo and fluffs up after being spun and knitted.

'extruded' and other synthetic fibres

There is an ever-growing group of fibres available to spinners, such as ramie (or nettle fibre), recycled plastic bottles and jeans and substances such as seaweed and milk.

Some are silky in appearance and some are not. The quality varies so ask for a sample first if you are buying by mail order.

The methods described in the section on silk tops, see page 178, can be used when spinning any 'silky' fibres and several of these will be looked at in more detail.

environmental issues

In common with a number of other synthetic fibres made from natural substances, soya silk is extruded using a chemical process. The chemicals cause some pollution, but then so does commercially scouring and dyeing wool. And, of course, both sheep and soya beans, like most things, can cause environmental problems if they are over produced. Sheep by over grazing and soya beans due to the use of land to grow a crop that is then exported instead of feeding the local population. Cotton causes problems due to the high rate of pesticides used when growing it and even organic cotton can cause concern about the amount of water used.

Using mostly fibres that come from near where you live and processing some fibre yourself, it is possible to reduce the environmental impact of spinning. Hemp is a good choice, because few if any pesticides are necessary for its production.

Ironically when buying yarn as opposed to fibre, people seldom give a thought to its geographical origin or environmental impact; one of the nice things about being a spinner is that you are closer to the source and therefore more likely to be aware of where the fibre comes from.

soya fibre

Soya fibre is exactly the colour of a cooked soya bean. It is a brighter shade of beige than Tussah silk. It is popular with vegan spinners who often choose to spin it instead of silk, because it has a similar appearance. It is made from the waste pulp left over from making soya milk and tofu, which is then processed and extruded in order to make fibre and is perhaps one of the nicest synthetic fibres available. It has more shine than the likes of bamboo and is less prone to pilling.

Soya is best spun from the fold or over the finger, just like silk but is a little more challenging so try silk first.

milk protein

This is another extruded fibre and comes in top form like many other unusual fibres. It is white and has a matt rather than shiny texture similar to bamboo. This makes it easier to spin than silk, soya or other shiny fibres.

bamboo

Bamboo tops and yarn are made from the fibres in the stem of the plant but it is chemically processed and then extruded much like other fibres in this group.

Quality bamboo fibre is 7.5-10cm (3-4in) long and surprisingly easy to spin. It results in a lovely, soft yarn ideal for baby clothes and luxury knitwear. It does not have much stretch or bounce so is not so good for large, heavier items. Add more twist if you want it to be hard wearing but some of the softness will be sacrificed.

seacell

Seacell is made from seaweed as the name suggests. It is another silk look-alike often with a colour best described as 'soft beige'. It is even shinier than silk and a bit more of a challenge to spin. The results are worth it though and it resembles the colour of Tussah silk. Seacell is a good choice for vegan spinners who want silk and with a more authentic colour than soya.

viscose and rayon

These were some of the first synthetic fibres to be developed for the textile market and predate even nylon and polyester.

More recently they have become available as fibre for spinners and are lovely. Both are made from wood pulp and are further examples of chemical processes being used to develop fibres. They are quite easy to spin and create soft yarns with low shine.

recycled fibres

Yarns made from recycled materials are fun to knit with and it is satisfying to spin old jeans, plastic bottles or knitwear! The processing still has some environmental impact but then everything does.

Fibre made from recycled jeans is of course a cotton fibre and usually available in blue. Recycled woollen fibre varies in quality and some can be quite coarse, so check carefully before buying it.

Plastic bottle fibre is very like polyester to spin and is usually available in white. It does not dye easily so this is a consideration when buying it.

Throwsters waste, pulled silk waste and sari silk are re-used waste rather than recycled fibres which is even better. These have been covered in the section on silk, see page 182–3.

Anything that is available as a knitting yarn is likely to become available as a fibre for spinners at some point and as spinning gains in popularity, yarn spinning companies find it worth their while to sell a wider range as fibres.

spinning fine yarns

There is a knack to spinning fine yarns and a few extra tips can make a big difference. Some spinners become real lace-yarn enthusiasts but fine spinning is something most do only occasionally.

It is not necessary to buy expensive equipment such as a lace flyer unless you really want to and any spinning wheel can be used to spin lace. Even a bobbin lead wheel such as a Louet can be used with some adaptation, though you may not manage ultra-fine lace on it and if you intend to spin lace regularly a bobbin lead wheel would not be the one to buy.

use good quality, very fine fibre

The traditional choice for lace spinning is Cormo fleece. This is not a breed as such but is a way of specially breeding Merino or similar breeds for extra fine fibre combined with a longer staple length. The fineness and crimp of the fibre are what defines it as Cormo. Merino or similar sheep breeds often produce fine fibre anyway but it can be variable and sheep that are bred specifically for the purpose give better fleece for fine spinning.

Fleece for fine spinning is usually available in small quantities from a specialist supplier by mail order. It can also be bought direct from suppliers in New Zealand, Australia, Tasmania or the USA. The international postage is not prohibitive if you live elsewhere, because you do not need much of it. Do not make the mistake of buying a whole fleece for lace spinning. Special fleece can usually be bought by the 100g and will be more suitable for the purpose. 100g goes a long way when spinning lace.

Follow the special instructions for washing Merino fleece, see page 140, and do not attempt to wash a large quantity at once.

Fleece is a bit easier to work with than tops, but extra-fine Merino tops are available from mainstream spinning suppliers. For fine spinning, buy tops with a higher yarn count – anything from 70s to 100s; the higher the number, the finer the fibre.

The neck wool from quality fleeces such as Shetland, Jacob and many others in the native or fine category can also be a good choice for fine spinning. Younger animals give finer wool, so first-clip wool or *hogg* fleece is the thing to get. Shetland is available in many natural colours and the colour variations in Shetland, Jacob or other rare breeds look wonderful in lace knitting.

It is satisfying to create lace yarns using fibre from near at hand, so explore the fleece available in your own country rather than assuming that Cormo is the only suitable fibre.

use mini combs

Mini combs are a great way to prepare fleece for fine spinning. They make small, open rovings that are easy to spin from and mean you do not have to keep joining new fibre on. They also prepare this delicate fibre without damaging it, which is a real risk if you use carders.

Remember to pre-draft the fibre if you are using tops and work from a small, narrow pencil roving pulled off the main roving.

clean that wheel

Oil and clean the wheel thoroughly before you start spinning lace, or the fine yarn will break. The hooks, flyer and orifice all need to be spotlessly clean and smooth. For details please see the *clean the wheel before you use it* section, page 57.

pad the bobbins

If you pad the bobbin cores (i.e. the centre part of the bobbin) it reduces the amount of pull there is on the yarn. A very fine yarn can break with the slightest jerk or pressure. The bobbins can be padded with foam pipe insulation. Or use a half-full bobbin and wrap paper around it to cover the yarn. Tie the paper in three places with some fine yarn to hold it in place, then spin on top of the paper.

fig 91: a padded bobbin; it has some spun yarn under the paper and will cause less pull on very fine yarn during spinning and plying

slacken off the tension

You need such a light touch when spinning fine yarns that the Scotch tension adjuster on the wheel is usually left off altogether, or laid over the bobbin end but not attached to the hook. Some people replace the Scotch tension spring with an elastic band as this gives less pull. If you are using a double drive wheel have the tension as loose as possible. Fine yarns were originally spun on double drive wheels and they work very well.

use the fastest whorl

Most spinning wheels have a series of whorls, with the smallest one putting the most twist into the yarn each time you treadle. Use the smallest whorl, because fine yarns need a lot of twist. If you have an older wheel with only one or two whorls on the flyer, buy a *high speed flyer* with extra whorls on it. This is worth doing whether you want to spin lace or not, as it increases the versatility of the wheel and will improve your spinning.

fig 92: different sizes of whorls; the smallest insert the most twist for the least number of 'treadles', some unscrew and some are fixed in place depending on the wheel

Many manufacturers make a lace flyer or a high speed whorl especially for spinning lace yarn and Louet offer high speed bobbins for their bobbin drive wheels. Some lace flyers require you to dismantle and change the whole flyer assembly which can be more bother than it is worth so check before you buy. Some are simple to change, like the one on my Timbertops chair wheel, which only requires taking one flyer off and putting the other one on.

A special lace flyer is only worthwhile if you are going to do a fair amount of lace spinning or want it to be ultra fine for competitions.

zigzag the yarn on the hooks

Another way to reduce the pull is to thread the yarn across the flyer from one side to the other several times rather than going up the hooks on one side. Then just use the three hooks at the far end of the bobbin. This is especially useful when using a bobbin drive wheel as these tend to exert more pull.

fig 93: the yarn on this flyer is zigzagged across the hooks to reduce the amount of pull when spinning fine yarn

fine yarns on a spindle

Support spindles are often used for spinning fine yarns, so that the yarn does not have to hold the weight of the spindle. A support spindle is actually any spindle that you rest on a surface.

A high top spindle can therefore easily be used as a support spindle, simply by placing the end on a slippery surface such as linoleum whilst you spin. This is very handy, as it means you can spin the yarn a lot faster. Remember to use a lightweight high top spindle and you will not need to support it all of the time. This means it will spin faster.

Being able to kick the spindle when you are using a high top is a great advantage, as fine yarns need so much twist. On a bottom whorl support spindle you could be twirling forever and still not get much spinning done.

A *tahkli* is often mentioned as a good spindle for spinning fine yarns on. It is actually heavier than most spindles, because it is usually made of brass or has a teardrop-shaped, heavy wooden whorl. It is probably the most tedious way to spin fine yarns and as a result, although quite a few people buy them, not many people use them regularly.

If you do want a support bowl the very best one is an upside down soft drinks can. See the section *support spindles* on page 31, with particular reference to Tahkli spindles, for more information.

put lots of twist in the yarn

Because fine yarns need so much twist, it is easy to get bored and feed the yarn in too soon. To test it, allow a section to double back on itself and ply. You should be able to see the two distinct strands plyed round one another. If you cannot, it needs more twist.

plying lace yarn

Ply the yarn carefully and make sure you insert enough twist when plying the yarn as well as when spinning the singles. It is very important that lace yarn is reasonably well balanced or it will snarl up and be difficult to work with. Remember that a balanced yarn is one that has the correct amount of twist in the plyed yarn to balance that in the singles.

Double back a section frequently and check that it looks plyed, rather than like two strands lying side by side. Add more twist in if in doubt. It is highly likely that you will under-ply a lace yarn and need to run it back through the wheel to insert more twist.

Counting the number of treadles you need per length of yarn is a very good idea for lace yarn, even if you do not bother when plying thicker yarn.

advanced plying techniques

There are two ways to get plyed yarn from only one bobbin of singles: Peruvian plying and Navajo plying.

Peruvian plying

Peruvian plying gives a two ply yarn from one bobbin or ball of singles yarn. It is equally useful whether using a hand spindle or spinning wheel and is widely used. It is a good technique if there is only a small amount of a particular fibre and you do not want to split it between two bobbins. It is also used for sampling yarn when designing.

It is important not to try the technique with too much yarn to start with, but as long as the yarn does not cross over itself when winding, once you have had a bit of practice it is possible to use a much larger amount. Some people have a slightly different method of Peruvian plying that means the yarn crosses and this is not the same as the method described here.

You can follow these instructions just the same whether you are winding the yarn onto the left or right hand.

securing the yarn

The end of the yarn is tied around the wrist in a half bow or tucked under a wrist strap, or both. Tie it firmly and leave a nice long tail because it is hard to find the end if it comes adrift.

The yarn is then wound around the hand in a certain pattern – you are actually using your hand as a special kind of *niddy noddy*. If you take the hand out and pull the yarn apart (not that you want to if you are plying the yarn) you will actually have a hank of yarn.

Follow the pictures and instructions on how to wind the yarn around your hand.

Please note: although it looks as if the yarn is crossed over in the centre, it is not. If you cross it over it does not work so well and it makes it hard to get your hand out.

Peruvian plying step by step

Get the spinning wheel ready with a bobbin in place or the hand spindle organised and ready to use before you start Peruvian plying. You cannot easily put the yarn down once it is wound onto your hand.

1. Tie the yarn around the wrist with a half bow, and leave a long end. Tuck the end under a wrist strap or elastic band if possible.
2. Have the back of the hand facing you. Take the yarn around the middle finger from the right hand side of your wrist and then take it back the way you came i.e. back to the right hand side of the wrist, without actually going around the wrist. In other words drop a loop of yarn over the finger.

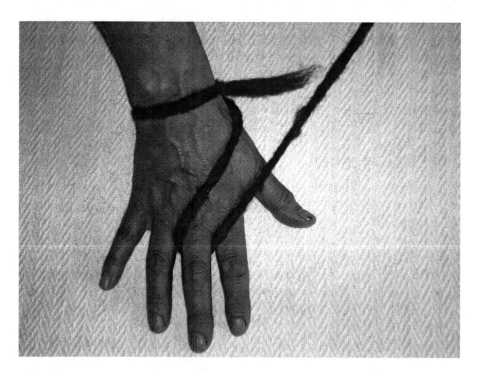

fig 94: Peruvian plying – make the first loop

3. The yarn now goes around the inside of the wrist – i.e. the palm side. And back to the front of the hand. It will now be to the left of the wrist rather than the right.
4. At this point you should have one loop around the middle finger that does not cross over itself. If you turn your hand over on your palm will be a 'ring and bracelet' of yarn. One loop on the middle finger and two around the wrist, including the yarn you tied around it to start with. This pattern will continue and at no time should the yarn cross the palm.

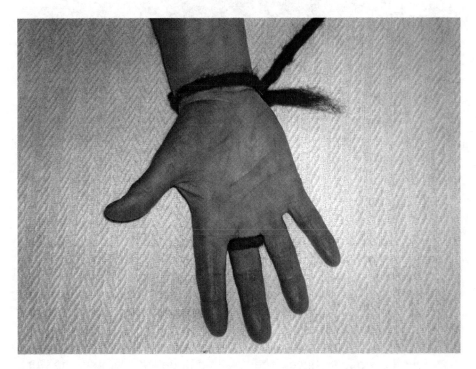

fig 95: Peruvian plying – the yarn does not cross the palm

5. Turn the hand round again so that the back of the hand is facing you and keep it like that. The yarn should still be at the left hand side of the wrist. Drop it over the middle finger, this time from the left and go back the way you came. The yarn has still not crossed over itself and is still at the left hand side of the wrist. Another loop has now been dropped over the middle finger, this time from the left.

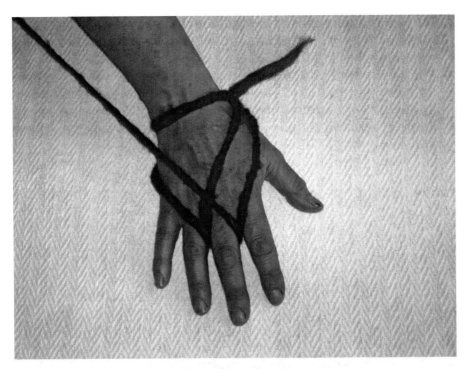

fig 96: Peruvian plying – *continue until all the wool is on the hand*

6. It will look as if the yarns have crossed over but this is because loop number one has crossed over loop number two. Just make sure it does not cross over itself when you actually make a loop.
7. Take the yarn around the inside of the wrist and back to the right hand side. You should now be back to where you started with the yarn coming from the right hand side of the wrist.
8. Take stock. On the palm side of the hand there should be two loops around the middle finger. There will be three loops around the wrist, including the original loop that you tied on. On the back of the hand there should be one loop over the middle finger to the right and one to the left. Each individual loop goes back the way it came but the two loops go in opposite directions so they look like they cross.
9. Continue in this fashion until all the yarn is wound onto the hand.
10. Keeping hold of the ends, break the yarn off from the bobbin. Untie the other end from the wrist and hold the two ends together. If you lose an end it is hard to find so hang on tight.
11. Slip the yarn up over the heel of the hand onto the palm, but do not take it off the hand. Keep your fingers through it at all times.

fig 97: slacken the yarn that is around the wrist in preparation for removing the middle finger from it

12. Now remove the middle finger from the loops so that it is through the yarn in the same way as all the other fingers. Do not pull the yarn apart and handle it gently or you will lose the 'cross' that the middle finger put in there. This cross stops the yarn from tangling.

fig 98: the middle finger has been taken out of the 'cross' and the yarn is now held loosely over the fingers in readiness for plying

13. Tie the two ends onto the shaft of a hand spindle or a fresh bobbin on the spinning wheel. Remember to thread them through the orifice of the wheel before you tie them on.
14. Ply the yarn, pulling it gently off your hand as you go. If it gets tangled, stop. The yarn has probably stuck itself together so just tease it apart. You should not need to put the hand through the two strands as you ply using this method but will need to if the yarn was crossed over itself whilst winding it onto your hand.

Navajo plying

Navajo plying creates a three ply yarn from one bobbin or ball of singles yarn. Like Peruvian plying, it can be done equally well on either a spindle or a spinning wheel.

Navajo plying is useful if you have only one bobbin of yarn and want to ply it to get a three ply yarn. Navajo plying is an easier and quicker way to make a three ply yarn than plying with three individual bobbins.

It is also good if the singles have turned out thinner than hoped, as the resulting three ply yarn will be thicker than two ply.

If you have spun a multi-coloured yarn, Navajo plying keeps the colours more separate than if two or three separate strands are plyed together.

a big chain stitch

Navajo plying is effectively a series of big chain stitches with twist in them. If you can do chain stitch – the foundation and most basic stitch of almost all crochet – then you are half way there. Getting started is the hardest part so persist and you will find it gets easier.

Navajo plying step by step

1. If you are using a spinning wheel, put the bobbin of singles yarn on a lazy kate on the floor beside you. If you are using a spindle (or if the yarn is already wound into a ball for some other reason) put the ball of yarn on the floor. It is not worth putting it in a jug as it will come out. Do not tie the yarn onto the spinning wheel or spindle yet.

2. Make a large loop in the yarn by laying it over itself. The loop should be 15-30cms (6-12 in) long. Hold the ends of the loop and the end of the yarn together (the ends that are furthest away from you) to stop the loop from coming undone.

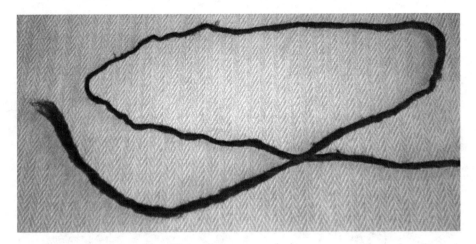

fig 99: Navajo plying – make a large loop

3. Reach through the loop with your other hand and pull a new loop of the yarn through the first one. This makes the first chain. Pull the loop through until it is nice and big.

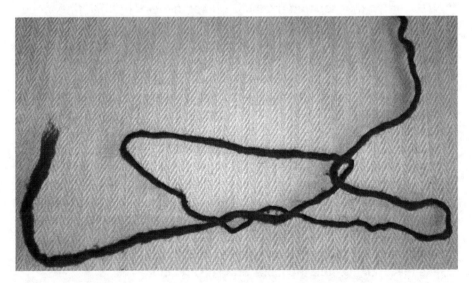

fig 100: Navajo plying – two loops: the second is made by pulling a new loop of yarn through the first one, just like chain stitch

4. Make a third loop by reaching through the second one and pulling the yarn through again whilst still holding the front of the loop and the end as at no. 2 above. The looped yarn should now be long enough to tie it on to the wheel or spindle. If not, make the last loop bigger.

fig 101: thread the loop and the loose end of the yarn through the orifice

5. Thread the end of the first loop and the end of the yarn through the orifice and yarn guide or hook and tie them onto the bobbin together as one, as if they were three ends. If using a spindle, tie the yarn onto the shaft of the spindle. It will now look like there are three strands tied on to the bobbin or spindle but there is really one strand and a loop.
6. Now treadle the wheel or twirl the spindle a bit to insert some twist. This will anchor the first loop so that it cannot come undone and it gets easier from now on. Do not let the twist travel all the way back into the unplyed yarn though because you need enough space to get your hand through each time to make the next loop. If using a spindle, it is much easier if you use your feet to twirl (or kick) the spindle as this leaves both hands free.
7. Reach through the last loop and make another one as before. Continue like this, making sure the loops are nice and large.

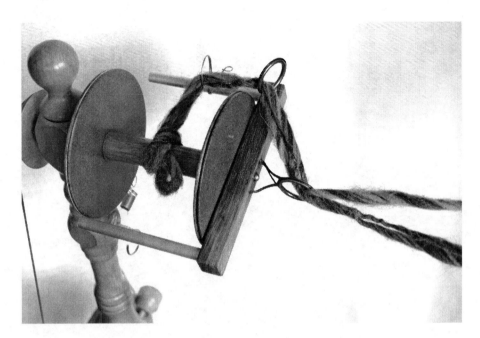

fig 102: tie them onto the bobbin core

8. If you are using a spinning wheel treadle slowly. On a spindle, use your feet or lower the spindle to the ground to stop it once you have enough twist. Take your time and do not try to keep the wheel or spindle turning all the time or it will overtwist. It is better to stop whilst you make the loops.

watch that twist

- It is easy to overtwist the yarn when doing Navajo plying.
- If it does get too much twist it will feel hard to the touch and may even get kinks in it.
- If the plyed yarn ends up overtwisted and all else fails, put the bobbin on the lazy kate or wind the yarn into a ball. Then re-spin it quickly going in the opposite direction i.e. untwist it a bit. Treadle quickly because you only want to remove some of the twist, not all of it.

This is a good tip with any overtwisted yarn and can be used on singles as well as plyed yarn.

finishing handspun yarn

It is best to wind the yarn into a hank and wash it once it has been spun. This relaxes the fibres and the yarn may actually become slightly thicker once it has been washed. Knitting or crocheting with unwashed yarn could mean you use too small a needle size resulting in a dense fabric with little drape.

Some spinners make samples of yarn when planning a project and these should really be washed to ensure they are the correct thickness. However although people talk about sampling and planning of projects a lot, the majority of spinners simply buy fibre that they like, spin it and then think what to make with it. That is fine – this is a hobby so do what you enjoy.

wind the yarn into a hank

This can be done around a large book or a picture frame, but a purpose-made *niddy noddy* works best of all and is inexpensive to buy. A niddy noddy is a special kind of skein winder that consists of two horizontal end pieces at right angles to each other, separated by an upright shaft. The yarn is wound around the niddy noddy in a zigzag fashion resulting in a long, neat skein.

Making one is not as easy as it looks, because the two ends need to be tapered just right so that the yarn is easy to slide off once you are finished but does not slide off of its own accord.

using a niddy noddy

There is no need to remove the yarn from the spinning wheel or spindle before winding it into a skein. Leave the full bobbin on the wheel but slacken the tension right off. A hand spindle can be put on the floor and left to roll around as the yarn unwinds. Trying to contain it is more trouble than it is worth.

1. Hold the centre shaft of the niddy noddy in one hand. Grip the end of the yarn in your hand along with it.

2. Use the other hand to guide the yarn and tilt the niddy noddy every which way to help you wind it over each horizontal end in turn. If it will not work, tilt it the one way that seems completely wrong because that's the one that is often right.

fig 103: winding yarn onto a niddy noddy whilst holding the end with the hand

3. The yarn goes up over one side of the top arm, down and round the
   bottom then back up to the top of the first one but over the other side of
   it. Then back down to the other side of the bottom one.

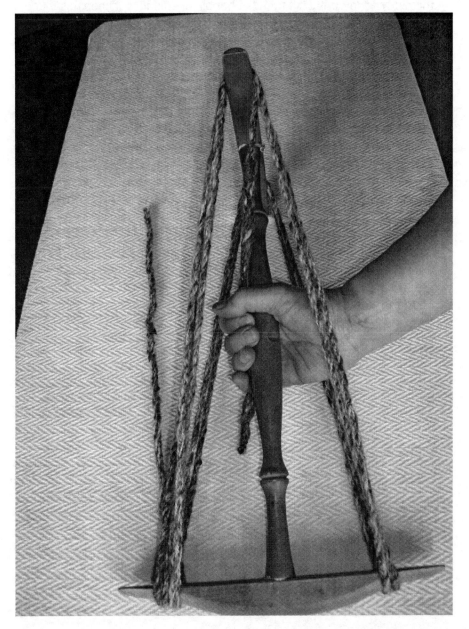

fig 104: wound yarn ready to tie; the hand is still gripping the first end

4. Once you figure it out, follow the yarn that is already there but take care not to cross over and go around the wrong side of the arm. Keep hold of the end as it is hard to find if you lose it. When all the yarn is wound onto the niddy noddy, detach it from the bobbin or spindle but keep hold of both ends and do not take the yarn off the niddy noddy yet.

5. Now tie the ends together. Take the yarn back to a point where they cross over and tie them in a single knot to start with. Then make a figure-of-eight tie around the skein with one of the ends. To make a figure-of-eight tie, work with one end only. Pass it under the skein of yarn but only half way and then bring it up through the middle of the hank. Continue to go round the skein but with the yarn now going over the top rather than underneath it. Go round the back of the skein and under it again up through the middle in the same place as before and bring it back to the front. Tie the two ends together but make sure the tie is loose with room for the yarn to expand. An overhand knot works well for this but use any knot if you do not know how to do one of those.

6. Break off three lengths of left over singles yarn and use these to put three further loose figure-of-eight ties in the yarn on the other three sides of the niddy noddy. Using singles yarn makes it easy to tell which tie has the two ends in it.

7. Slide the yarn off one end of the niddy noddy to remove the hank.

fig 105: figure-of-eight tie on a hank of wool

how to wash the yarn

Opinions vary on how to wash handspun yarn. I like to give it the hottest wash it will ever have before it becomes a garment because the yarn will usually shrink a little and I would rather it did that before I make it into something. For the same reason I do not block or stretch yarn. There are people who do not wash yarn before using it and those who swear by blocking. As you gain more experience you will see what works best for you.

To hot wash yarn, add some detergent to water as hot as your hand can stand and drop the yarn into it. Any liquid detergent, shampoo or washing up liquid will do. Do not move it around or change the temperature of the water suddenly or it may felt.

Once the water has cooled, rinse the yarn but make sure the temperature of the rinse water matches the cooled water that you just took the yarn out of. Fabric or hair conditioner can be added to the final rinse if desired.

Squeeze the yarn dry in a towel or put it in a pillow case, tie the top and give it a light spin in the washing machine. Hang it up to dry but do not block it. The one exception is when yarn is being spun for a show or competition. You may want to block it in that case either by hanging a towel through the hank or by putting it back onto the niddy noddy to dry, although you should remember that wood may stain damp, pale-coloured yarn.

using handspun yarns

Handspun yarn can be used in the same way as any other yarn – you can knit, crochet or weave with it, spin fine silk threads for embroidery and yarns for canvas work, stitched or woven tapestries.

The main problem you will encounter as a beginner is that you do not have much control of the thickness of the yarn you produce. At the start, the best projects for handspun yarn are therefore things that either do not have to fit or are small in size; a scarf, hat or cot blanket are good projects for a beginner. Small items do not vary in size as much as larger ones if the yarn is a different thickness to that suggested in the pattern.

It is easy to make up your own simple patterns. For a scarf or cot blanket, estimate the number of stitches and knit or crochet a few rows to see how it looks. If it is too wide or too narrow start again and alter the number of stitches. The size is not crucial anyway so long as it is not vastly over- or under-sized. Add a stitch pattern such as a moss stitch border to a knitted cot blanket and do stripes in different colours. I have included a couple of basic patterns here in case you are daunted by making up your own.

a scarf

Cast on the desired number of stitches depending on needle size and the thickness of the yarn. A loose tension makes a softer scarf so use large rather than small needles. Narrower scarves are more comfortable than wider ones, especially for children.

If the scarf is knitted in garter stitch, rib or moss stitch it will not curl up at the edges. Add different coloured stripes as you go, taking care to change the yarn on the same side each time for a neater look.

To do *rib*, knit one stitch and purl the next one but make sure a knit stitch is always above another knit stitch and a purl stitch above a purl stitch. Do the opposite to get *moss stitch* i.e. a knit stitch goes above a purl stitch and vice versa. An even number of stitches works best for rib and an odd number for moss stitch. You can also do knit two, purl two rib or moss stitch, plain knitting with a cable up the middle or anything else you fancy.

To crochet a scarf use double or treble crochet and change colour as desired.

Any scarf can be finished by adding tassels. To make these thread four or so strands of yarn at a time through the ends of the completed scarf with a needle. Double them back and cut them to length, then tie each bundle with an overhand knot. Space them out along the ends of the scarf so they are not too close together or they will distort the knitting or crochet.

a cot blanket

Cast on the required number of stitches. This will depend on the thickness of the yarn, the size of the needles and how large you want the finished blanket to be. It is not crucial so an estimate is fine.

Knit stripes in different colours of yarn if desired, either randomly or with an equal number of rows in each colour. You can also add little pattern motifs across the stripes, such as alternate stitches in a different colour across one row every so often.

to make a moss stitch border
Knit a few rows all in moss stitch at the beginning of the knitting following the instructions above. Alternate the two rows, always making sure that a purl stitch is above a knit stitch to get a textured look.

Once the border is large enough, continue in stocking stitch (unless you want a blanket that is all moss stitch) but do moss stitch for about 10 stitches at the beginning and end of each row so that the border continues up the sides. At other end, do all moss stitch again for the top border and cast off.

samples help to get the size right

By checking that the scarf or cot blanket is the right size and starting again if it is not, you have in effect knitted a *sample*. By deciding on the stitch pattern, needle size and colours you have also done some basic knitting design. This stuff does not need to be complicated or scary.

For larger items it is common to knit a sample square. With small items that do not have to fit anyway, it is often not worth the bother.

Because handspun yarn is different to commercial yarn, many spinners start making up their own simple patterns and get better at it over time without really noticing.

how to adapt a commercial pattern

Commercial crochet and knitting patterns give details of how many stitches and rows there should be over a certain size of sample square – usually about 10cm (4in). To adapt a pattern to your handspun yarn, start by choosing one that is for yarn of approximately the same size as the handspun.

Knit a tension square larger than four inches – a six inch square makes it easier to measure the four inches accurately – and the larger the square the more accurate the tension. For chunky yarn do a bigger square – the chunkier the yarn the larger the square should be. Count the number of stitches and rows you have to the inch and compare this to the advised tension for the pattern.

When using thick yarns there is a smaller margin for error because the stitches are larger. A counting error of half a stitch with a tension of 3 stitches to 2.5cm (1in) is a lot of extra inches in a 90cm (36in) sweater. An error of half a stitch with a tension of 20 stitches to 2.5cm (1in) is much less.

If the knitting or crochet needs to be smaller, go down one or two needle or hook sizes and if it needs it be larger, go up in size. This is often enough and avoids the need to do calculations.

If calculations are necessary, it is often easier to make up your own simple pattern. This is especially true of anything that has a surface design such as Fair Isle or lace knitting. Alternatively go back to the section on control of thickness in spinning and practise some more. Then spin yarn that is closer to the correct thickness, knit a tension square as before and adjust the needle size if required.

how to design your own garments

Almost anything can be made from squares or oblongs. Knit a hat from two squares and sew them together. Turn up the brim and put a tassel on each corner. Or sew the corners together and put a pom pom on top. Make a drop-sleeved, slash neck sweater by knitting one oblong for the front, another for the back and one for each sleeve. Make it into a cardigan by making two oblongs half the width for the front and one of full width for the back. Sleeves are actually about the same width as the back and front on the average sweater. Before you know it, you will have decided to decrease at the cuffs and add a bit of neck shaping – and are designing without noticing.

If you want to take it further there is an excellent book on knitwear design called *The Sweater Workshop* by Jacqueline Fee, see *resources* page 219. I found it easier to follow than other books on the subject and it teaches knitting design in a way that requires no sewing up.

there is a whole other world out there...

In his book *Scenes from a Smallholding* Chas Griffin tells the story of his wife learning to spin. With her beginner's yarn she knitted him a rather substantial, muddy-brown-coloured jumper with a knitted cable up the centre front. He tried it on and when he asked his wife how he looked, she replied 'you look as if you have been run over by a moped'.

Thirty years ago most spinners were spinning only fleece, mostly in the grease, and when you were taught to spin that is about all you learned. Handspun garments often looked, well, grungy and a bit odd – even the ones in spinning books. The yarn could be pretty solid and jumpers for larger people weighed in at a couple of kilos. These days they are exquisite. If something looks handspun it is by design rather than mistake.

There are many aspects of spinning that it is impossible to do justice to in one small book. Some of the things that have been covered, such as fine spinning or spinning silk, could be the topic of a complete book in their own right. We have not looked at spinning cotton and linen, colour blending, or spinning fancy yarns and these are topics to explore in the future. Then there are the related worlds of dyeing, weaving, knitting, crochet and rearing fibre animals. In other words you never run out of things to learn.

Finally, do not let any book tell you there is only one way to do anything. It is good to learn the 'right' way but once you know the basics, experiment. And you soon learn that for every book that says one way is right, there is another that says the opposite! All the techniques we have today came about through experimentation.

resources

organisations

The Association of Guilds of Weavers, Spinners and Dyers

www.wsd.org.uk

The British Wool Marketing Board

www.britishwool.org.uk
01274 688666
a good source of fleece and educational products about wool production

suppliers

Create With Fibre

Janet Renouf-Miller
Ayrshire, Scotland
www.createwithfibre.co.uk
mail@createwithfibre.co.uk
01292 550393
workshops on spinning, knitting, crochet and dyeing, hand-dyed fibres and
yarns and books on spinning and dyeing

Previously published booklets by, and available from, Janet:
Spinning Fancy Yarns
Natural Dyeing
Learn to Knit (also available as a kit with yarn and children's knitting needles)

Scottish Fibres

Near Edinburgh, Scotland
www.scottishfibres.co.uk
sales@scottishfibres.co.uk
0131 445 3899
a mail order supplier with a range of fibres, books, spinning wheels
and looms including Louet and Ashford

Twist Fibre Craft

Fife, Scotland
www.twistfibrecraft.co.uk
enquiries@twistfibrecraft.co.uk
01337 842843
a range of fibres, knitting yarns and spinning wheels, they have a shop in Newburgh, Fife, Scotland and also do mail order

Once a Sheep

Gourock, Scotland
www.onceasheep.co.uk
karen@onceasheep.com
01475 648089
a knitting shop that has a large range of knitting yarns and sells spinning wheels and looms

World of Wool

www.worldofwool.co.uk
an online supplier of fibres that sell good value 'bin end' bags of mixed fibre

P and M Woolcraft

Milton Keynes, England
www.pmwoolcraft.co.uk
01908 510277
a range of fibres, books and spinning and weaving equipment including Lendrum

Wingham Wool Work

South Yorkshire, England
www.winghamwoolwork.co.uk
wingwool@clara.net
01226 742926
a mail order supplier of fibres, equipment and books, Winghams are also fibre processors on a small scale and suppliers of English wool combs and blending hackles

George Weil and Co

Guildford, England
www.georgeweil.com
01483 565800
a supplier of fibres, dyes, looms spinning wheels and other supplies

Ashford Handicrafts Ltd

Ashburton New Zealand
www.ashford.co.nz
sales@ashford.co.nz
+64 3 308 908
makers of spinning wheels and looms, Ashford can advise
of suppliers in your area

Louet

Holland
www.louet.nl
+31 573 252229
makers of spinning wheels and looms, Louet can advise of
suppliers in your area

David Bryant

www.craftdesigns.co.uk
instructions for making spinning wheels and some metal parts

courses

LILI

www.lowimpact.org
01296 714184
LILI has a range of over 1000 courses, including spinning,
at different venues all over the UK

Janet Renouf-Miller

author, provides workshops and courses; please see full details on page 219

books

These books are available from LILI's online bookshop,
www.lowimpact.org/manuals.htm.
LILI also sells books on most other craft and environmental issues

Spinning and Weaving at Home

Thomas Kilbride, Thorsons, 1980
buy it direct from the McBrides at
Croft Wools and Weavers
Ri-Aulidh, Cuaig, By Applecross, Strathcarron,
Rosshire, Scotland IV54 8XU

Through the Eye of a Needle

John-Paul Flintoff, Permanent Publications, 2009

The Sweater Workshop

Jacqueline Fee, Interweave Press, 1983

places to visit

The Highland Folk Museum

www.highlandfolk.com/
01540 673 551
Aultlarie Croft, Kingussie Rd, Newtonmore
Invernesshire PH20 1AY, Scotland
this museum covers a huge area and has various buildings, farms and
antique buses to ferry you from place to place. It has spinning and
weaving demonstrations as part of the live rural life exhibits.
Admission is free

Macclesfield Silk Museum.

www.silkmacclesfield.org.uk

Ashford Handicrafts

www.ashford.co.nz/newsite/
415 West Street
Ashburton, New Zealand
Ashford has a studio and visitors are welcome

other LILI publications

Learn how to heat your space and water using a renewable, carbon-neutral resource – wood.

This book includes everything you need to know, from planning your system, choosing, sizing, installing and making a stove, chainsaw use, basic forestry, health and safety, chimneys, pellet and woodchip stoves The second edition has been expanded to reflect improvements in wood-fuelled appliances and the author's own recent experience of installing and using an automatic biomass system.

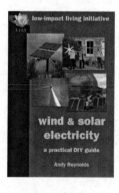

The author has been providing his own electricity from the sun and the wind for many years, and in this book he explains how you can do the same.

There are chapters on the various system components required (including inverters and charge controllers), how to put them all together, batteries, grid-connected systems, and there is even a basic electricity primer. Andy has analysed the output of his system for over 10 years, and these real-life figures are included.

The author grew up in Jamaica and was taught to make soaps by her grandmother. They grew all the plants they needed to scent and colour their soaps and even used wood ash from the stove to make caustic potash.

Her book is intended for beginners, includes both hot- and cold-process soap making, with careful step-by-step instructions, extensive bar, liquid and cream soap recipes, full details of equipment, a re-batching chapter plus information on the legislation and regulations for selling soap.

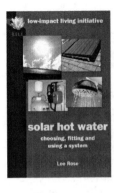

solar hot water: choosing, fitting and using a system provides detailed information about solar-heated water systems and is particularly applicable to domestic dwellings in the UK.

Lee Rose has 10 years of experience and involvement in every aspect of the solar thermal industry in the UK and around the world. His book provides a comprehensive introduction to every aspect of solar hot water: including all relevant equipment, components, system design and installation and even how to build your own solar panels.